Happiness Starts With Gratitude

50 Gratitude Lessons to Direct, Inspire & Empower You

Volume 1

David George Brooke

The Brooker – That Gratitude Guy

David George Brooke

ISBN-10:1482789027
ISBN-13:9781482789027

DEDICATION

My deepest gratitude to my late wife
Dana, who gave me two incredible sons:
Connor and Kyle

David George Brooke

CONTENTS

David George Brooke

ACKNOWLEDGMENTS

Mark Victor Hansen, James Malinchak, Viki Winterton, Michael James, Michael Charest, Kody Bateman, Patrick Snow, Katherin Scott, Sara Boren, Robert Crosetto, Terry Simpson, Steve Leith, Nancy Juetten, and Mark Herdering

1

Daily Gratitude Journal

Hi! It's the Brooker, "That Gratitude Guy." I thought it was time to do a real quick update of how and why you write in your Gratitude Journal. Well, actually— you know why—but I'm going to tell you how. So here it is, the Brooker's Daily Gratitude Journal. It has a very specific structure to make it kind of easy to follow. Basically, every single day, you have your Gratitude Today on the left side and your Gratitude Tomorrow on the right side. So it starts with, of course, the day and the date and then your daily number. As I've mentioned in the past, the daily number is something I feel very strongly about. It's one through ten. Ten is maybe one of the best days of your life and one is one of the toughest days of your life.

That daily number in the upper right hand corner of the left hand page is what anchors how you're feeling that day. You can go back and look at the events and see what's happened. It's very important to sort of assess yourself, if you will; you can refer back to that number and so forth. It kind of gives you a feeling for where you are for that day.

Next, there are the current events and special occasions . . . just a couple of lines. That's basically there to let you talk about anything that's going on in your life. You don't have to have a diary or another journal; you can do it all here in the Gratitude Journal.

Now, "I'm so grateful for" . . . that's everything you're grateful for today. In particular, you start with the most important things in your life: your health, your children, your family, your friends and so forth.

Then we have the highlight of the day – one of my favorites. What's the best thing that happened to you yesterday or, if you write in your journal towards the end of the day, what's the best thing that happened to you today? And then there is a little quote. It's different every single day, so that you can refer to it, and it's always something about gratitude.

Then, on the right hand side and very important, your gratitude intentions, otherwise, called "gratitude tomorrow."

"I'm so grateful for something that is going to happen that hasn't even happened yet" . . . because your brain cannot distinguish between what actually has happened, and what's going to happen, so you write as if it's already happened. "I am so grateful for the fact that I'm going to graduate with this grade point average" or whatever it might be. That's how that works.

For those of you who would like to get a Gratitude Journal, I highly recommend it. Go to thebrooker.com and look for the icon on the right hand side; it takes you right to Amazon. Once you place your order, it will be there in 3 or 4 days.

Then go to my email, which is thebrooker@thebrooker.com. Email me, and in the subject line, put "Gratitude Journal." Give me your name and address and I'll send you another gratitude journal completely free; I'll even pay for the shipping. It's a great gift idea. The journals last about three to four months. It's nice to have one ready to roll when you get to the last page on your current one.

As I have said so many times, the transformational powers of a Gratitude Journal are unbelievable, but you have to experience it for yourself as you deal with life and all of those ups and downs that come along the way. So, get yourself a Gratitude Journal. I would love it if it was mine, so go ahead and take advantage of that offer. You'll see what a difference it makes. Have a grateful day.

David George Brooke

2

The Power Of Gratitude

Today's topic is "The Power of Gratitude."

September 29, 1998 . . . that was the day that my wife passed away, a very, very difficult day, to say the least. I started to look for ways to cope. In fact, we live in a world that has nothing but stress, and nothing but pressure. We all need healthy coping mechanisms. Now, there are many, many unhealthy ways to cope with stress–drugs, alcohol and pills— you name it, and they're not very healthy. There are all sorts of ways that people try to cope, to try to numb the pain, to get away from the pressure of life.

The gratitude journal has changed my life. It gave me that seven-and-a-half, eight minutes a day to focus completely on what I was grateful for. Look at what gratitude can do. There was a recent survey in the restaurant business. It showed that when members of the waiting staff wrote "Thanks" on the customers' receipts, tips increased by fifty percent. When restaurant staff welcomed customers when they arrived, and, as they left, said "Thanks again for coming, I really appreciate it," the average tip went up, and the average experience improved.

Now, I've been talking about this for years. It took me almost 40 years to finally figure out what I was going to do with my life. It came to speaking about gratitude to groups, and spreading this message—specifically, the idea of a gratitude journal. The power of gratitude is immense and, once you start on that gratitude journal, you will see things manifested every single day, every single week, every single month, that will be just unbelievable. When you start thinking about what gratitude can do for you, and where it can take you, you won't believe it.

Just remember, have a grateful day—and don't forget to write in your gratitude journal. Take care.

3

The Day That Changed My Life

I'm going to talk about a day that changed my life. It was September 29, 1998, a Tuesday. I woke up and my wife was not there. I couldn't figure out where she was. So I got my son, Connor, and we started looking around the house, walked down the hallway, looked in some of the rooms, but we couldn't find her. Finally, we looked downstairs, and there she was . . . on the floor. Something was definitely wrong.

Connor started screaming. My 14-year-old son, Kyle, got up. He started yelling. We called the ambulance, the police, the fire department; everybody came. They started working on her, but something was dreadfully wrong. As you can imagine, I was very upset and when something like this happens, time goes at a very, very different pace.

There must have been fifteen people in the house with all of the fire, police and the EMTs that were there. One of them, a young lady, told me, "We've been working on your wife for an hour-and-a-half and we still don't have a heartbeat. Would you like us to continue?"

Well, needless to say, even in a state of shock, I knew that she had passed on. As time froze and the days went on, it was very, very hard to deal with the fact that my 38-year-old wife was dead, and my four-year-old and 14-year-old sons no longer had a mother, and I no longer had a wife. It was very difficult, as anybody who has gone through a trauma of this nature knows.

Ultimately, I found gratitude. And gratitude is something that has altered me for the rest of my life—changed me, helped me, encouraged me, and probably—in fact, for sure—saved me. What I want to talk about in this book is how gratitude can change your life. As I've said when I speak to groups, gratitude saved me, and it can save you too.

As those days went on, I was searching to find ways that I could go forward, as well as try to be the best father possible to Connor and Kyle. There were days when it was really a struggle. At some point, I ultimately found a gratitude journal. That gratitude journal really made it possible for me to put my grateful and appreciative thoughts, if you will, on paper every single day.

So I would like to encourage you to connect with my website. It's http://www.thebrooker.com You can purchase my gratitude journal there. You can learn about my upcoming speaking events, and about other books that are available for purchase.

In upcoming chapters, we're going to talk about many other aspects of gratitude that can help save you, by allowing you to refocus, and reframe your life as something positive. So if you've had something bad happen in your life, or there's something you've really struggled with, like depression or any number of other things, please consider gratitude and please consider a gratitude journal.

So, remember to visit me at thebrooker.com and to take care.

David George Brooke

4

Sharing Gratitude

Today's subject is "Sharing Gratitude." I'd like to share a little story about what happened to me some years ago. I've been a pilot for many years, and so I've had the chance to log a number of hours in an airplane – enjoying many very, very memorable experiences. Let me tell you one story about something that happened to me along the Oregon coast.

I was flying along using VFR flight rules (Visual Flight Rules are followed when you can see everything around you; Instrument Flight Rules mean you can be up above the clouds and in between cloud layers.) I had contact with the ground and, all of a sudden, I went between cloud layers. It was a little bit scary, but I thought, well, I think I can handle this, because I've had enough hours and I'm a pretty good pilot.

As I flew, suddenly something crazy started happening. The sun came in from the side and these colors hit the clouds above me and the clouds below me. They were surrounding me and I must have been going a hundred and forty, a hundred and fifty knots ground speed. It was just like this light storm of every color in a kaleidoscope – above and below – and I was just hanging on for dear life. I thought it was like something out of a movie, like Space Odyssey 2001 or something, and I just held on.

It seemed like five minutes, but it probably was thirty or forty-five seconds in reality. But all of a sudden, I popped out the other end. My eyes were still as big as saucers, and I came out and there were blue skies and clouds. And I still was hanging onto the yoke for dear life because it just felt like something I never experienced before. And I caught my breath and I looked over and said, "Wasn't that cool?" and then I thought, "Oh, I'm by myself."

So after all these years, I never got to share that story with anybody else, and I realized that sharing is what makes stories and life experiences so valuable. Nobody ever got to see that kaleidoscope of color except me. There was nobody else I could share it with, because I was flying by myself.

So remember, when you embrace gratitude, when you understand gratitude, when you write in your gratitude journal every day, and express that gratitude and appreciation for your life and for the people that are close to you, and your job and the roof over your head and so forth — remember to share it. Pass it on.

Express your gratitude to other people, to your passenger who, in my case, wasn't there, but is maybe sitting next to you. Write in that gratitude journal and I promise it'll change your life.

5

Make Room For Gratitude

Today's lesson is about clearing out your brain and making room for gratitude. So what am I talking about? When we want to make a change in our lives, it's like spring-cleaning – we've got to get things cleaned out to make room for new things coming in. When I talk about gratitude coming into your brain, and expressing gratitude, and understanding gratitude, and writing in your gratitude journal every day, you've got to make room for it.

So let's see if you're the kind of person that can change. If you are, excellent. If you're not, you're not alone; it seems like for every twenty people I talk to, maybe one can really change. That reminds me of a story.

There was a young lady who worked for me years and years and years ago. Her name was Sandy. She was always saying that I was telling her the same thing: "Are you the one or are you the nineteen that aren't going to change?" She said, "Mr. Brook, I'm the one that can change. I promise I'll change." She promised that she was the one who was going to completely change her life. I said, "Great."

Unfortunately, she became pregnant and moved back East to where her mother was. And she said, "Listen, I'm going to clean up my life." She'd had kind of a tough life. I think maybe she'd been in some occupations that weren't exactly the best. It hit some tough things when she said, "You watch. I'm going to make this change. I will be that one and not the nineteen." I said, "Okay."

So she moved and about a year later, I got a call: "Mr. Brook, it's Sandy." "Hey Sandy, how are you doing?" "I just want to let you know everything worked okay. I'm the one." She said, "I had my baby." I said, "Great and a little boy or a little girl?" "Yup, a little boy." I think it was Bobby or something. "And how's he doing?" "Great." "And how are you doing?" "Great. I completely changed my life. I'm the one and not the nineteen."

I asked her what else is happening. "Well, I have a new boyfriend and he's really a fantastic guy." And I said, "That's wonderful. What does he do?" "Well, he's on work release right now." "Uh, okay." Well, Sandy certainly tried but I wasn't sure that was the right path for her to be on.

But it's so important to remember, when we want to

change our lives, we've got to start with ourselves. We've got to say, "Am I the one or am I the nineteen?" We are the ones that can say, "I'm going to clean out my brain, get it ready for gratitude, start being grateful every single day, writing in that gratitude journal, thinking about all the positive things I have in my life."

But you've got to clean house first. Clean out the room, if you will, to make space for the new gratitude that's coming in.

So that's today's lesson. Have a grateful day and don't forget to write in your gratitude journal. Take care.

David George Brooke

6

Bit by Bit

I want to talk about gratitude as it relates to taking things a piece at a time, bit-by-bit, bite-by-bite. Now what I mean by this is that a lot of what we've talked about is how gratitude can help you propel forward, refocus and reframe everything in a more positive way.

Well, what about what happens when we have something that's a little overwhelming? What happens is it seems like that there's a certain mountain out there that's just too high, too cold, and too snowy, whatever it might be.

It reminds me of a story I've thought about for a long time. We had a nice fireplace and I needed to order a cord of wood. In fact, you know what, let's make it two cords of wood.

So the wood is delivered. It's a gigantic pile. I have never seen anything so big in my life. I believe a cord is $4' \times 4' \times 8'$. This wood completely filled the driveway – eight feet high, eight feet wide, and sixteen feet long. So, it's this giant pile of wood. I worked on it. I didn't make a dent. I was very discouraged, I was cold, I had slivers in my hand, and I thought, "what the heck is going on here?" Forget it. I'm just going to do this later. I'll never get it done. I'll have to hire somebody — you name it.

But then I thought, "wait a second here." Let's think about this as a bit-by-bit, bite-by-bite type of thing. I went inside. I got rid of a couple of the slivers. I got some nice warm gloves. I got a cup of coffee and a radio with my tunes. And I just started carrying pieces back and forth. I didn't really think about it. I had the nice warm gloves on, no more slivers. I took the logs inside, put them into place, and went back and forth, back and forth.

Lo and behold! All of a sudden, an hour and a half later – it didn't even seem like it – both cords of wood were inside, dry, stacked neatly where they are supposed to be and ready for the fire.

I thought about that later. I call it the cord of wood theory, because you cannot take on something when you're looking at it in its enormity. If you look at that big mountain out there, it seems really huge.

They say that every journey starts with just one step. Well, working on those two cords of wood, it was just one piece at a time. As you're looking at your life, refocusing, reframing, looking at everything from a grateful perspective, make sure you're just looking at it bit by bit.

So, that's today's message. Don't get it too big – chunk-by-chunk, piece-by-piece – that will help. Remember I'm The Brooker at thebrooker.com. Have a grateful day. Don't forget to be writing in that gratitude journal. Take care.

David George Brooke

7

I Want to Play the Drums

All right. Today, of course, I want to talk about gratitude. But I want to talk about something else that's been a theme of mine for my entire life. Never, ever giving up. I believe that it was Winston Churchill who said it first, "Never, ever, ever give up."

What I'd like to talk about today is something that happened when I was about 12 years old, in fifth or sixth grade. I decided that I wanted to learn how to play the drums. I just thought that'd be such a neat thing to do. So I signed up.

The form asked if I wanted to play the drums. The second question was "what do you want to play after drums?"

"I don't want to play anything else. I want to play drums."

"Well, you have to put something else down."

"Okay."

"Alright. Put down trombone." So I wrote down trombone.

Anyway, I had to wait in line. I was so excited because I'm going to be a great drummer some day. I'm going to take my lessons and go on to be a real well-known drummer. I was just so excited about it.

The teacher called me up to the front, I walked up to the counter and gave her my card. She says, "Okay, you want to play the drums." She takes a pencil and goes —tap, tap-tap-tap-tap, tap-tap, tap-tap.

"Now, do that."

Okay, that didn't seem too hard. Tap, tap-tap, tap-tap, tap-tap-tap, tap-tap.

She says, "Trombone for this boy!"

Well, I never got to play drums. I did play the trombone. I wasn't very successful at that. I tried the guitar. I had a little bit of success with that. But I've had many other successes in my life and the reason is because I just flat refused to give up. In the last chapter, I mentioned the cord of wood theory – don't look at the enormity of it. Don't look at those two gigantic cords of wood; break them into bite-sized pieces.

But I remember that I was so set on playing drums

and it just didn't work out that way. But other things worked out really, really well. Along the way, I realized that I have to be grateful for the skills I have. Apparently, my rhythm skills weren't as good as they should have been and it was "trombone for this boy!" Well, that might crush some people, but it didn't crush me. It just made me have that much more resolve to do other things.

So, please remember, be grateful for the talents that you have. Embrace them, rejoice in them, and refocus and redirect your thoughts to the things that you're good at; as I once heard somebody say "Make your strengths productive. Make your weaknesses irrelevant."

So that's it for today. Please remember to write in your gratitude journal every single day. Take care.

8

Everything Happens For a Reason

Here's what I want to talk about: everything happens for a reason. I know not everybody believes that, but I believe it to be true. I've had many, many examples in my life when something happened and later on, I found out the reason. So let me share a brief story with you. Frankly, I am grateful that these types of things happened to me, because once again, they helped me reframe and refocus my life by realizing that things happen for a reason.

When I was growing up, I had three brothers and a sister. We used to just pound on each other. It was just sort of a normal upbringing with all five of us. My older brother, he used to just beat the you-know-what into my head. He'd get me down, put his knees one on each of my shoulders – just pound my face in. I remember thinking: some day I'll be bigger than him and I'll be able to get the best of him (which did happen later, but I digress). So, whenever we'd get in a fight, my mother would always come and break it up, bring us together and say "Alright you two, I want you to hug each other, say you're sorry, and tell each other 'I love you'."

I would do it . . . it didn't matter who started it, who was winning. I'd put my arms around my older brother and I'd whisper in his ear "I love you. I told mom I love you. I'm going to kick your you-know-what when she leaves the room."

As we went through the years, I wondered why my mom always had us do that. Well, years later, when I was in my 30s, my mom contracted abdominal cancer. Unfortunately, she was only around for another year but I remember when she died. There were four, five of the hospice nurses and us, all huddled around, holding my mom and cradling her head. It was 7:05 on a Monday morning; she took her last breath and the hospice nurse turned to the five of us and said, "She's gone."

And as you might expect, especially those of you who have lost parents, my three brothers, my sister and I started crying and kind of hugged each other. Then, all of a sudden, those 25 or 30 years of hugs made sense to me. Because here were those same brothers and sister that I had fought with and had had to hug and tell "I love you" and "I'm sorry", who were feeling the same pain I was. Sharing that pain, those hugs made sense. That proved to me once again that everything happens for a reason.

So that's something I believe. I'm very grateful for that. I'm grateful for having those brothers and sisters and I'm grateful for my mother for making sure that we did hug each other and tell each other that we loved them.

So that's my story for today. Be sure you're writing in a gratitude journal every single day for seven and a half minutes. Take care.

9

The Shoeshine Stand

Today I want to talk about, of course, gratitude. What a surprise! But I want to talk about being grateful for who you are and how you express that to other people in your life. I'd like to share a little story with you, called The Shoeshine Stand.

For many years, I worked in the downtown area. There was a shoeshine stand across the street, located inside a coffee shop. There was a nice young man there, actually named David, the same name as mine. And I would go there and get my shoes shined maybe once a week or a couple times a week, whatever, and I got to know Dave real well. In fact, the guy was so incredibly bright and intuitive, I used to say "I don't know which got a better shine, my shoes or my brain."

But one day we were just talking about people in general and he said, "You know, Dave, do you realize that kind of all the Who's Who of our town come here to my shine stand?" He named some of the best known – the mayor, the captains of industry, some of the well-known names. He was very, very familiar with these people in our city.

He said, "Do you know, Dave, what they all have in common?"

I said, "All motivated?"

"Yes. But that's not what I'm thinking of."

"Very driven?"

"Yes. But that's not what I'm thinking of."

"Passionate – really believe in what they're doing in their business and how they are part of our city?"

"Yes. But that's not what I was thinking of. Anything else?"

"What is it?"

And he says, "They never talk about themselves."

And I thought that was such a powerful message because I remembered people telling me: "If you really want to find out about somebody, what they're like or what they are made of, if you will, ask somebody else. They never talk about themselves." So be very grateful for who you are, what you are, the skills that you have, the things that you are proud of.

But remember that when you're chatting with people, it's best for you to learn about them. Let them find out about you from somebody else.

And again, be grateful for who you are because that's what it's all about.

We're going to talk more about gratitude. Be writing in that gratitude journal every single day – left-hand side, what you're grateful for today, right-hand side, what you're grateful for tomorrow.

10

95 mph Fastball

For today's topic, I want to talk about gratitude.

Gee, that's a surprise. But I want to talk about how it relates to your attitude. The — "if you think you can, you can; and if you think you can't, you can't."

Now, I was thinking about this whole discussion, about how we should be grateful for the skills we have, and not worry about the things we don't. Be very thankful for those skills that you bring to the table, make them important in your life, and make the skills you lack irrelevant. This reminds me of a story.

I was talking to a good friend of mine, Maximo, and we were discussing our local baseball team. And we asked each other, "Don't you think you could hit a 95 mile an hour fastball?" And we looked at each other and went, "It's probably not real likely." But then we decided to go down to the field, find a way in, ask one of the pitchers to throw us a couple of 95 mile-an-hour fastballs and we'd each take our shot.

So Maximo and I talked about it and said, "Here's the thing. You could get the bat out in front of the ball and maybe get a bloop single. Maybe you could get a bunt. Maybe the ball is coming so fast that you just stick the bat out and see if you can get a bunt or something that would be counted as a single, but at least you'd get it. You'd get the shot and you'd have a chance; it might be very small, it might be one-tenth of a percent or half of one-tenth or what have you, it might be very, very small, but at least you have a shot. But if you never go to the field and you never take a swing at that 95 mile-an-hour fastball, there is 100% chance you won't get a hit."

So why not apply that to your life? Always give it that shot, even if the odds are long. It's like what I've said about looking in the distance and seeing a mountain. Let's not talk about how high the mountain is and how cold it is, how much snow there is . . . let's talk about getting our snowshoes and a map; let's get the equipment that we're going to need, let's talk to somebody about the best way over the mountain. Let's figure it out because attitude and gratitude really are almost synonymous. So when you think about how grateful you are, think about your attitude and remember that it'll really, really take you a long ways.

And just remember, the next time somebody asks you if you think you can hit a 95 mile-an-hour fastball, just go down to the ballpark. At least you have the chance.

So that's today's chapter. I'll see you tomorrow. Remember to be grateful every single day and don't forget to write in that gratitude journal. Take care.

11

Change in an Instant

Okay. So for today's lesson, we want to talk, of course, about gratitude and thankfulness and appreciation. But also about how, in many, many ways, if you're very in touch with who you are and how you think, you can change your behavior in an instant.

In an earlier chapter, we talked about getting over a mountain. Are you going to discuss how high, how cold it is, or are you going to discuss what route you're going to take, and what equipment you need? So think about that and about how quickly you can change behavior. That brings to mind a story.

Years ago, I was working for a big retail chain and I had started to move my way up. And one day, somebody kind of called me aside. He said, "You're getting a lot of press, if you will. Around you, people are talking. You're getting nominated for Department of the Month. And the word on the street is that you think you're pretty hot stuff," he added.

I went "Wow, really?" and asked, "How so?" "Well, when you walk around, you don't talk to anybody. You have your little briefcase when you're marching through the store and going to your department and so forth. And you're not very friendly and so on."

And it really hit me. I said, "Well, thank you for passing that on to me." And I realized that if I was going up the escalator and said "Hi!" to somebody, or waved and asked someone "how are you doing?", or "how's your department doing?", the escalator didn't move any more slowly. It didn't make any difference.

I realized right then and there that as I'm walking along, with my little briefcase, acting like Mr. Important, I'm not going to move any faster and it's not going to get me there any quicker than when I actually say "Hi!" to somebody as they're walking by.

So from that moment, it was *Snap!* – literally like that. I realized you need to be a lot more open, more friendly, and pay attention to other people, and I changed my behavior. Don't just be in your own little world. But my biggest message is being grateful for the skillsets you have and for having a brain that's open-minded so you can change behavior like that. You don't have to tell somebody, "Well, I'm working on it. I'm going to try to do better." Just like Nike said, "Just do it." It's so true.

You can change in an instant. From that moment forward, I had a much different attitude. And I think it came across a lot better, a lot more humble, if you will, and more as part of a team instead of "Mr. Busy carrying his briefcase around."

So just remember that; if you're thinking about your gratitude, think about your appreciation, your thankfulness for all the skills that you have. But remember, you can change just that quickly.

Don't forget to write in your gratitude journal every day and take care.

12

974 Toothpicks

We've talked about a lot of interesting ideas, breaking things down bit by bit and piece by piece, being really grateful for everything you have, and, if you think about your skill set, not worrying too much about what you don't have. Today, I want to talk about something in more detail, and I actually have a visual aid.

I want to talk about being grateful for every challenge, every obstacle, and every hurdle that you have overcome in your life because you are able to break it down into little bit-by-bit pieces. I talked about that earlier. But today, I'd like to discuss an example that I think really makes the point.

If you look at the graphic, is that a 2 × 4, a standard cut piece of wood used in construction that you see, or is it 974 toothpicks? You decide. There are the 974 toothpicks, and there's the 2 × 4.

The reason I mention this is because so many people seem to think a 2 × 4 is just one big thing when, in fact, it's 974 toothpicks that make up that 2 × 4. So think about everything that you're really grateful for in your life. Think of all those 974 little pieces that made you that single unit that you are today and be grateful for them. It's so important to remember that we must embrace everything that we're happy for, everything we are grateful for, and everything that we do that's good, and not worry about what we're not good at.

So let's remember to pay attention to that every day and make sure that when you write in your gratitude journal, you think about those little itty-bitty things that are so important. Are you grateful for just being healthy, feeling good – all the arms, the legs, everything works? Did you get a good night's sleep? Did you have a hot shower? Were you able to have a good meal, or two or three meals today — those things that we take for granted? So make sure you're remembering every one of those little 974 things that add up to that 2 × 4 and you'll be even more grateful today, tomorrow, and then in your future.

Remember, gratitude today on the left-hand side, gratitude tomorrow on the right-hand side. Take care.

13

Let the Day Come to You

We just came off the three-day holiday weekend. A lot of people think "Gosh, I've got to get a lot of things done; I've got to accomplish this; I've got my to-do list; I've got to do my chores and so on and so forth" – and that's fine.

So you're asking, "Well, just how exactly is that related to gratitude." Well, let's talk about this for a second. How about if we look at it a little bit differently? How about instead of actually going through the list, doing everything you better make sure gets done, and getting that sense of accomplishment that a lot of us feel, we're just grateful for just having the time to reflect, to relax, maybe enjoy the family, and appreciate the three-day weekend.

A term I like to use is "Let the day come to you." Years ago, I thought "Gosh, I've always got so many, many things I have to do." And I thought, "How about if I just sit back and relax. Instead of —having a to-do list, the grocery list, I got to do the yard, and

I've got to do this — how about if I allow the day to come to me?" The whole concept just takes a little bit of pressure off and it's actually perfect because it really encourages gratitude.

Think about this . . . "let the day come to me. I'll think about how healthy I am. Maybe it's a beautiful day out. How about family? How about all the things in my life that are really, really good?" And just sit back a little bit. Have a cup of coffee, a cup of tea. Whatever it might be, let the day come to you because, remember, we're constantly looking for ways to think about all the things we're grateful for.

And when we are on a holiday weekend, a day off, whatever it might be, it's a perfect time to sit back and just let the day come to you, just letting things flow. It gives your mind a good chance to think about all that's good.

We're constantly bombarded with negativity. You watch the news, you read the papers, you listen to the radio, whatever it may be, negative, negative, negative, everything that's wrong in this world – the economy, the wars, you name it.

So here's a chance to sit back and just reflect on everything that's good in your life. So the next time you have a day off – a two-day weekend, a three-day weekend, a holiday weekend, whatever it may be –

let the day come to you.

Please remember to write in that daily gratitude journal – it will do wonders, it will change your life – seven and a half or eight minutes a day. Everything you're grateful for today on the left-hand side, everything you're going to be grateful for tomorrow, your gratitude intentions, on the right-hand side.

Take care.

14

Fighting Depression

I want to tackle a subject that is kind of near and dear to my heart. I'm going to talk about how gratitude can help something that affects a lot of people every single year, every single day – in many cases, minute by minute – and that's depression.

I had the unfortunate happenstance of having a mother that suffered from depression. I remember when I was growing up, sometimes depression was called feeling blue, feeling down, under the weather, gray, — all sorts of ways to describe being depressed. And I think I probably got pieces of that from my mother along the way.

But I noticed in the world where we have all sorts of ways that we cope, so many of our coping mechanisms are negative or destructive – there's drinking, smoking, drugs, pills, gambling. There are all sorts of ways that people try to numb themselves from the pain. And when I started really developing this gratitude journal, not only writing one myself but also developing one for others, I noticed a huge difference. And this has not only become an excellent way to remove obstacles and get things to clear in your head, but it also can really, really prevent feeling down.

It's something that I noticed when I talked about how to use The Brooker's Daily Gratitude Journal. Every day, we have gratitude on the left side for gratitude today and gratitude tomorrow on the right side. But also there's our daily number and I noticed that number kind of affects how you feel for the day. Ten is maybe one of the best days ever and one is a pretty tough day.

But I've noticed every time I have a tough day, feeling down or anything, I grab this journal, sit down, grab a pen, take that seven and a half to eight minutes and start writing down everything I'm grateful for and that number always goes up. Certainly, this is no substitute for seeing the doctor to diagnose the depression, i.e., clinical depression or anything that's extremely important or extremely tough to deal with, but it certainly does help.

So keep that in mind and try it out. I urge all of you to get a Brooker's daily gratitude journal. Start writing in it every single day – seven and a half to eight minutes is all that it takes – and see what happens, especially on those days that life's a little bit tough. And your number, your daily number, will probably pop up one, two, or three places. I've seen it happen to me and I just think this is such a great way to have a healthy means of dealing with a world that has so many unhealthy, destructive coping mechanisms.

A lot of people are trying to numb the pain. Here is a way, writing down every single day the things that you're really, really grateful for. It may be something simple like just taking a hot shower and having a warm bed to sleep in versus that homeless person who has nowhere to go.

So keep that in mind. Keep writing that journal every single day and see if it works for you. I promise that you'll see some really, really good results.

Have a grateful day and take care.

15

The Starfish Story

Today, I've got another story about another aspect of gratitude. I want to talk about how gratitude can affect the entire world.

Now, some of you may have heard this story before but if you haven't, it's well worth repeating. It's called the Starfish Story and it talks about the impact we have on people, one person at a time.

As the story goes, two gentlemen are walking along the beach at low tide and all these starfish are up on the sand. Of course, the tide is way out, the sun is beaming down and the starfish are just getting fried. They're going to die if they sit in that sun for much longer.

So, as the gentlemen are walking along, one of them is talking when the other guy stops, reaches down and picks up a starfish. His friend asks what he's doing. He says, "Hang on a second." He cranks up his arm and throws the starfish back into the ocean. His friend says, "What are you doing? What difference will it make?" And he replies, "It will make a difference to this starfish." *Bam*! And the starfish goes out into the ocean.

So that's why I wanted to kind of change the tone and talk a little bit about gratitude as it relates to one person at a time. I've given many talks to service organizations, Kiwanis, Chambers, Rotary, schools, you name it. There are always a few people that tell me that I've just changed their lives with the way I talk about gratitude. Sometimes, they've got tears coming down their cheeks and they say, "I liked the story that you told about this, how you survived by using gratitude."

That one starfish that went out into the ocean got saved. So let's think about that. What if you change one person's life by telling them about gratitude, about how they should think about everything that they're thankful for, make their strengths productive, their weaknesses irrelevant, and about writing in that gratitude journal every single day?

If you can change just one person that day, that will make such a difference. They say every great journey starts with just one step. But let's not forget that, like that one starfish back in the ocean, you saved that starfish today.

So remember to spread the word about gratitude.

There's nothing that will make you feel better. Start by setting the best example; start by writing in that gratitude journal every single day, embracing gratitude, thinking about everything you're thankful for. And then pick up that starfish, pick up that friend, give him a little bit of encouragement, talk about what he can be grateful for and, believe me, it will make a huge difference in your life.

Take care.

16

Do It Right

Okay. Today I want to talk about doing it right. And when I think about doing it right, I think about a couple of sayings I've heard over the years. I worked for a large retailer, a very prominent retailer in town, and actually a national retailer. One of the best things they ever taught was, "Do it right or don't do it at all."

I also thought about that old saying, "You never get the second chance to do it right the first time." That was another one that really hit me. You get one opportunity to do it right the first time. And another one I heard recently was, "Do you want it right now or do you want it right?"

So when I think about doing it right, of course, I'm talking about gratitude and the gratitude journal. I give talks. I speak and I sell the gratitude journals. And people say, "Well, how would that change your life?"

I say, "Well, listen. One of the big things about this

is you've got to be consistent with it every single day." In fact, they talk about "Here is the routine. Get out of bed. Take a shower. Brush your teeth. Get your clothes on. Write in your gratitude journal."

But be sure you do it right. A lot of the comments that I get are, "Well, I kind of get it occasionally right. I think grateful thoughts and, gosh, they're kind of random. I'll try to do better next time."

I say, "Well, listen, don't do it for me. Do it for yourself."

One of the things I said early on is that when you think about it, it's like a dream. When you talk about it, it inspires you. But when you write about, it empowers you. And that is very powerful, very, very powerful.

This morning, I was in a coffee shop. I was putting my daily entry into the gratitude journal. This guy looks at me as I'm having my cup of coffee and writing this. "Wow, somebody is actually writing something." And I said, "Yes, you can't do it on a Word doc. You can't dictate it. You've got to write it down. When you write it down and you're doing it right and it's 'I'm so grateful to be as healthy as I am, I am so grateful for the two sons I'm so blessed to have, I'm so grateful for the roof over my head,' there is something about the way it connects to your brain that makes a huge, huge difference."

So remember when you're writing in your gratitude journal, when you're speaking about gratitude and, for that matter, for your whole life, do it right. And just remember – do it right or don't do it at all. I thought that was a very, very good message.

Have a grateful day and, of course, be writing in that gratitude journal. Take care.

17

The Company You Keep

For today's discussion, I want to talk about, of course, gratitude, but I want to talk about another aspect – and that's the company you keep.

Think about the people that affect you in your life, who you hang around with and how they impact you. So, if you're writing in your gratitude journal, if you're writing every single day about all the things that you're grateful for — you've heard me say before: if you think about it, it's like a dream; if you talk about it, it inspires you; and if you write about it, it empowers you — if somebody looks at you and asks, "What are you writing? What's all that kind of stuff?" and they're negative, think about how that's going to impact you and think about the people that you are letting impact you in your life.

Now, I'm one of the most positive people you're going to meet. I've had a lot of tragedies, a lot of trauma in my life, but gratitude has really saved me and delivered me to a place of appreciating everything that I do have and looking at what's good in my life and not what's bad.

I was having a cup of coffee with my dad and we got talking. Unfortunately, he was very negative. And he was complaining and complaining about just about everything. We were just sipping on our coffee and I looked over at my dad. I said, "You complain a lot," and he goes, "Did it ever occur to you I might just like to complain?" It kind of sunk in for a few minutes and I said, "Did it ever occur to you I may not want to hang around you?"

So it can be family. In my case, it was my own father but it can also be friends. It can be your peer group, your co-workers, what have you. Watch who you will let impact how you feel about things.

I was in a seminar a couple of days ago; it was kind of a Mastermind group about businesses and promoting businesses. And I just thought, wow, what a bunch of incredible like-minded people. I thought just how much it brought me up and really got me inspired. And that brought me back to thinking about how we let people affect us. I thought that if you wanted to learn how to swim, you might want to ask Michael Phelps. That might be a good thing to do.

I thought about a guy I worked for years ago when I was in college. I was working for a local bookstore and he was my manager. He had a little neatly worded sign and I used to look at the sign all the time and laugh at it. I was 19 or 20 years old and it wasn't until years later that it hit me what that sign meant. It said:

> You meet respectable people where respectable people gather. If you're looking to find mountain trout, don't   go fishing in a herring barrel.

Well, years later, it still made me laugh, but the message was much clearer. If you're looking for mountain trout, what are you doing fishing in a herring barrel? It's a great point.

A close friend of mine once said, "I had many friends that have become acquaintances," because they weren't aligned with his way of thinking. So remember, when we're talking about gratitude, be proud of embracing gratitude; be proud that you're writing in a gratitude journal. Remember, be writing, not typing Word docs and not shorthand and not speaking into a microphone – pen in hand, writing in that journal. Embrace it and be aware of who's around you. And just remember that you're certainly known by the company you keep and that they can bring you up or they can bring you down. Hopefully, the people you're hanging out with will bring you up.

So keep writing in that gratitude journal every single day. It will make a difference, a huge, huge difference in your life. Have a grateful day. Take care.

18

What Time of Day?

What I want to talk about today is "What Time of Day?" and by that, I mean, "What time of day are you writing in your gratitude journal?" I'm assuming you all have a gratitude journal by now. If not, I'll talk in a little bit about how to get it and why it is so important.

When I first started out, I always wrote in the morning. And I thought, "Well, that's going to set the tone for the day" because when you get it right, what you're grateful for today, and what you're going to be grateful tomorrow, sets the tone for the whole day. But later I noticed that I was up very early in the morning and that didn't really work out too well, so I started writing midday, which didn't work too badly. It gave me the chance to stop in the middle of the day and really reflect after I already had been at work for a couple of hours.

Later, I talked to some folks that were doing it before bed. Now, I am one of those people who are very fortunate in that they sleep pretty well. But I think if you have trouble sleeping or if you had a busy day and you take a few minutes to reflect at the end of the day, that may be the best time for you. Just before bed sets your mind up to really relax, be in a grateful mood, think about everything you appreciate in your life, everything that you have that is good. And the petty or negative things tend to fall away.

I think all of us have woken up in the middle of the night with just all sorts of things going around in our heads. Those times that's happened to me, I have actually gotten up and written them down. It's never quite as many as I thought but still it's amazing how when you're trying to sleep those little thoughts can get in your head and really cause problems.

So, morning is probably my preference. As I've said many times: get out of bed, take your shower, brush your teeth, get your clothes on, and write in your gratitude journal. So if that works, great, that's the perfect time of day for you. If midday works better, that's fine. Or if it works best right before you go to bed, that's fine too. But make sure you're writing.

Now, for those of you that haven't had the chance to get a journal, go to http://www.thebrooker.com and you can order right there online. It covers about three to four months, seven and a half to eight minutes a day. I promise you it will change your life.

So remember, whatever time of day you decide works best for you, start doing it immediately. You'll see huge, huge results. All right. Have a grateful day. Thanks a lot. And again, take care.

19

Practice What You Preach

As always, today's topic is of course centered around gratitude. But what I want to talk about today is the concept of practicing what you preach. Now, of course, I'm going to relate it to gratitude, but I also want to talk about the example that we set in our personal and our business lives and as parents. I happen to have two sons. How do we set that example?

And I think back on how my parents raised me, the example that they set, that they practiced what they preached. As a parent, as a boss, are you having people do exactly what you do instead of just what you say? The same thing is true with gratitude.

I had a career that involved managing a lot of people in several big retail operations and I remember getting these questions a lot: "How come everybody respects you? How come nobody respects me? What is it about being a good leader?"

And I would consistently hear: "I'll never forget

when you said this, Mr. Brooke. — You're the first store manager we had that ever took the time to do .... — You're the only person who's ever done this for us, sir." Or "You pitched in and rolled your sleeves up and helped out." It is all around setting a good example, leading by example and practicing what you preach. So let's bring that back to gratitude.

I think with gratitude – again, I mentioned this in an earlier lesson – as you're writing in your gratitude journal, don't worry what other people think. Think about the example you're setting for your peers, for your family, for your children, for your friends, for whoever it might be, and show them by doing it yourself, leading by that example, practicing what you preach as you write every single day about your gratitude and intentions start to manifest themselves in all these good things that will happen to you.

I've mentioned some of the amazing things that have happened to me in the last four or five years when I was grateful for something that was going to happen but hadn't happened yet – and then it did. I was so grateful for different things in my life, like I had gotten away from focusing on again about being healthy mentally, physically, financially, emotionally, and spiritually. All these ways because we get so caught up in all the negativity.

So remember to practice what you preach. Be grateful every day. Lead by example. Set that example with your gratitude, practice it every day, and especially with your gratitude journal.

Now, I've talked a lot about making sure you're writing that every day. If you haven't had the chance to pick one up yet, the website is http://www.thebrooker.comand you can also reach me by e-mail at thebrooker@thebrooker.com. So that's today's message. Keep working hard, keep writing in that gratitude journal, have a grateful day, and take care.

20

Managing Stress

We're going to talk about a subject that's near and dear to my heart, certainly about gratitude, but centered on managing stress. It's so important that we manage our stress. Life is very stressful. We've got to keep things in perspective.

I was thinking about this one day and I thought about how we can manage stress, and certainly gratitude is a huge, huge piece of that. But it's always about keeping things in perspective and that's one of the big things that gratitude will do and specifically, of course, writing in the gratitude journal – it helps keep things in perspective.

I'm sure you may have heard that story about the man who said he felt bad because he had no shoes, until he saw a man who had no feet. So it's always about keeping things in perspective. And if you don't, one of those things is stress, which can kill you.

I remember a doctor buddy of mine once said

obesity, drinking, smoking — all these other things combined, all these bad habits that people get into as they try to cope with life, all combined — will not do as much harm as stress will.

I thought of a story that's kind of related to how you have to manage your stress and manage your perspective and keep things in check, if you will. I've been a pilot for many, many years. Years ago, I was on a flight to the ocean with my wife and another couple when we got caught up in a storm.

It got really scary. We turned around to head back and all of a sudden, I was panicking. I was pulling up on the yoke and the stall horn started to go off which meant the plane was going to stall. I could feel my little heart beating. I was not managing the stress at all well. I thought this could be the end. I decided to look over and I think I'm in a straight level, but I'm in a 60-degree bank turn to the right.

I remembered what my instructor said – don't ever panic. Always remember what you were taught. Always think clearly. Take a deep breath. Take an inventory of your thoughts, if you will, and pull it back in and manage the situation.

Fortunately, I was able to straighten out the plane, lower the nose and keep climbing up through the clouds – it was very, very frightening – an instrument situation. To make matters worse, it was at night. Gosh, it must have been 15, 20 minutes later that we broke through the clouds at 10,000 feet. I remember thinking that I was so glad I'd caught myself and was aware of it.

There was another time when I was scuba diving; the mouthpiece started to pull out and I was getting half water, half air and I started panicking. I remember back then thinking, "Hold on. Think about what's happening to you now. Think about it. Don't panic. Make the assessment."

Then I put the mouthpiece firmly back to my mouth, cleared out the water and started breathing. I was very much in a panic situation, but I got control of it.

So think about that. Always keep it in perspective. Be aware of the situation. And something that will make a huge difference in turning it around is gratitude. Think about gratitude. Think about the things that you're grateful for. Your perspective will change, just like the gentleman who had no shoes and saw the gentleman with no feet.

Write in that gratitude journal every day. If you need a gratitude journal go to http://www.thebrooker.com. I highly recommend it. Seven and a half to eight minutes a day will completely change your life and refocus you. It refocuses your brain, and reframes the picture to something of a much more positive nature. So manage that stress. Remember it can just absolutely change your life, and I promise that gratitude journal will make a big difference. Have a grateful day. Thanks a lot.

21

It's Never Too Late

Okay. You've heard me talk about never giving up. I've sometimes felt that was kind of part of my life story, the traumas and tragedies, the things I had to overcome by never giving up. But I want to take it a step further today, and that is to say that it's never too late. It's never ever, ever too late. So I just want to give a couple of examples.

I remembered going to a local lake that the people would run around. I'd always see a gal who was running and who was kind of heavy. I'd be kind of starting to snip at her like "Look at her. She's so....." And then I'd think, wait a second, wait a second, David. She's doing something about it. It's never too late to get in shape. It's never too late to get gratitude. Let gratitude help you in your life. It's never too late to restart and do something different tomorrow.

In fact, I remember reading some years ago that just because it didn't work yesterday doesn't mean it can't work today or tomorrow. So think about all the people who have never, ever given up.

Sylvester Stallone apparently went to tons and tons of people trying to get financing for Rocky before he was finally successful. He never gave up and it was never too late for him. Walt Disney had a tough time finding financing for Disneyland and all that he did after that, but he never gave up. It was never too late.

And I think my favorite is probably Col. Sanders who, in his mid-60s, decided to take his special herbs and spices and put together this chain that would later become KFC; of course, he was very successful well into his 80s and 90s.

I'm 62 years old. I had the idea at 19 I wanted to be a motivational speaker but I never knew what I wanted to speak about. It seemed like a lot of people were motivational speakers.

Well, it was several years ago, half a dozen to be exact, that I found gratitude, and it transformed me, which is why I want to speak and do speak so often about gratitude, and having a gratitude journal. That's why I write these lessons to explain to people the power of gratitude. But it took me over forty years to find that message of what I was going to be speaking about. But I never gave up and it's never too late.

So remember that. Write in that gratitude journal every single day. It will transform your life. Don't give up. Always hang in there. And trust me, you will get tremendous results. Have a grateful day.

22

Be True to You

All right. Today, what I want to talk about is being true to yourself. Now, pretty much everything I talk about revolves around gratitude, but there are different elements that we can take out of our lives, apply to gratitude, and see how they will change, and impact, and really enhance our life.

I was thinking about being true to yourself because I thought about how I used to exercise a lot. I realized that I would go out and run sometimes when I felt like it, but every time my friend came and I heard those two knocks on the door, I got up and ran. I always upheld that commitment to him but not necessarily to myself. And because I noticed that, when he didn't come knocking at the door, I might or might not run, I thought, "Was I really being true to myself?"

I thought, "What is it about your making the commitment to somebody else but you won't make a commitment to yourself?" So the same thing goes for the gratitude and specifically, the gratitude journal. I have people ask me all the time, "How does the gratitude journal work out for you?"

"It works out great."

"Well, I don't really do that. I think about things. I say my gratitude out loud."

I reply, "That's fine. I'm just telling you and I'm going to say it over and over and over again: If you think about it, it's like a dream; if you talk about it, it inspires you; but if you write about it, it empowers you."

Really think about that person you see in the mirror every day and be true to that person.

I remember going skydiving. It was many years ago and there were about six of us. We all signed up and everybody was all excited. We decided to go in our separate cars and just meet there at the skydiving place. Perfect. So I go there and I'm waiting and waiting and pretty soon I realized nobody showed up except me.

I thought "My gosh, it's just me." The instructor came out. "Where's all the group?" "Gosh, I don't know. I guess they had a flat tire and they couldn't make it or something." But, yes, I was there. I was true to myself and it was a great experience, by the way. It was a static line jump. It was a lot of fun, scary but a lot of fun.

So be true to yourself. That's the message today. Think about that when you're brushing your teeth, just before you're writing in that gratitude journal. Take a good look at that person and ask that question: "Are you really being true to yourself?"

You can see me at http://www.thebrooker.com - that's my website, and you can email me at thebrooker@thebrooker.com. Have a grateful day. Keep writing in that gratitude journal. I'll see you later.

23

Gratitude for Veterans

Okay. I want to talk about something a little bit different and put a slightly different twist on things today. Last week was Memorial Day. I want to talk about gratitude for veterans. Where would I be, where would all this be without the people that are in service to our country?

Now, I did not go into the service. I had a father and a couple of brothers that did. But every single day I write in this gratitude journal, and I talk about how grateful I am to be healthy, how grateful I am to have a roof over my head, how grateful I am to have a nice place to sleep, and a good meal, or a couple of good meals, every single day and so forth.

But where would I be without our veterans? I think of my father and my brothers that served, many, many friends of mine that served, and about the several friends I lost in several wars. We have several wars going on right now.

Let's remember every single day to be grateful for all

our veterans, the people that served for us. I think, God, it's so hard to imagine where we would be without them. And again, when I'm talking about being grateful for the roof over my head, and being healthy, and so forth, that's just great, but where would that be without our freedom?

I thought back about, gosh, I was a young boy. I was climbing a cliff and was very, very high above a huge bridge and the ocean was down below. As I was climbing, I got to a point where I couldn't climb any more. I couldn't go up and I couldn't go down and I was really, really scared.

And I remember there was a guy up above me that I had kind of forgotten about, because I was so afraid. And as I kept climbing, the rocks were crumbling. I was way, way above the ocean level – probably a thousand feet or so. I don't know how I got in this predicament, but as I reached out to grab another rock, everything crumbled and this guy's hand comes out of nowhere, grabs my wrist, and pulls me to safety. Now, I never knew who that person was but, basically, he saved my life.

The reason I mention that story is, when we think about service from others, and service in our country, probably the greatest service of all is that of the men and women that serve us every single day. As I mentioned, we have several wars going on right now. So let's remember to be very grateful for our veterans. I'm going to do a better job of putting that in my gratitude journal every single day, because it's that important, and I don't want to ever take them or it or any of that for granted, because it's something that has saved our country, and I'm so appreciative and so grateful to our veterans.

That's it for today's message. Take care and have a grateful day. Please don't forget our veterans. Be grateful for them, and I'll see you tomorrow. Take care.

24

Friendships

Today, I want to talk about, as always, gratitude but especially gratitude around the subject that I think a lot of people think about sometimes, and that's friendship. And I think about friends I've known for a couple of weeks, a month or two, and then I've got friends that I've had for over 40 years. In fact, I used to joke that I've got friends I haven't even used yet.

But I think what is so important is that we think about the value of friendships. Recently, a book came out titled *The Five Regrets of the Dying* and they said "I wish I'd had the courage to live a life true to myself, not the life others expected of me," "I wish I hadn't worked so hard," "I wish that I had let myself be happier." And one of the five was "I wish I had stayed in touch with my friends."

Friendships are not only something that are very powerful socially, but also affect our income. I saw a survey once that related friendships to the economical aspect of our lives. This survey found that your income will be 75% of the average of your five closest friends.

I think that it is important to remember the value of friendship. Again, back to the book about *The Five Regrets of the Dying*. People talk a lot about this as they get older: make sure they exercise, make sure they stay active, stay involved, and make sure they stay hooked up and in touch with their friends — very, very valuable.

I frequently write in my gratitude journal that I am so grateful for the friends I've had, for a month or two, for several years, and several of my fraternity brothers and good friends I've had for over 40 years. Those friendships are very, very valuable.

I even think about how, in order to stay in touch, we should always take the high road. Make that call, send the e-mail, and send that text; check in just to say "Hi!" You'll be really glad you did.

On a regular basis, write in your journal about how much you appreciate those friendships, because there's something about sharing, just like sharing gratitude, that makes it so much bigger and better for all of us.

So that's it for today. Have a grateful day and we'll talk again later. Bye!

25

Ups and Downs of Life

Of course, we're going to talk about gratitude but our discussion is always about something that relates to gratitude and how it can kind of tie in with the rest of your life. Now, I want to talk about the ups and downs of life.

For years, I've wondered why we wake up some days fired up, everything is great, cooking on all eight cylinders if you will, everything is falling into place, maybe the weather is nice, everything you know is working in your favor, and then there are other days it's just the opposite.

And you look and you think, "Well, how did I sleep? What did I eat? Did I get some exercise? Is it biorhythms?" Who knows? There are all these factors that contribute to how and why we have an up or down day. So gratitude and the gratitude journal is such a big part of it.

I realized that a lot of it's kind of like a progression and you have to stick with it. They say that all the journeys start with the first step. I ran a marathon once. I didn't think in terms of 26 miles; I just thought of it in terms of a mile, taken bit by bit.

I remember when my brother called me and said he had bought a hydroplane. He wanted to learn how to race it and at some point, I thought, well, maybe I'll be involved. But I just said, "You know what, can I just try it just once? Can I just drive it?"

He goes "well, sure." So I went out and drove it. It was real scary. It went very fast, about 100 miles an hour.

And then later, I followed him around as he was racing. I said. "Do you think I can just take it out on the course just once?"

And he goes, "Yes, sure." So I took it out on the course, got the helmet and the driver's suit. I went around the course and I was pretty excited.

And then eventually I did that a few times. I asked if I could be entered in one of the heats if I stayed in the back and out of the way. He said, "Sure." So I did that and continued on. Eventually, I got into racing with him and ultimately, we became National Champions.

And I thought about all the steps that I went through to get to the point of being a National

Champion – from the very first time when I was so scared that I just wanted to drive, but not be by any other boats, or anything like that. And I thought that really kind of feels what life is like – it's step by step by step. You wouldn't meet somebody, go out on a date and say, "How about tomorrow we get married?" It always goes through all those steps.

So remember, when you're dealing with these ups and downs of life, include the gratitude journal as one of those key components, no matter how you're feeling. I use a one to ten scale in the gratitude journal, ten being my best day, one, a not so good day. And no matter what number I wake up with or no matter what number I feel I'm at, at that time, I write it in that gratitude journal. It always pops up one or two or three steps or one or two or three numbers.

So, if you will, remember that. Have a grateful day and don't forget to be writing in that gratitude journal. Take care.

David George Brooke

26

Stay Healthy

Today I want to talk about staying healthy. Whenever anybody talks about staying healthy or being healthy, they so often think of eating right, getting your sleep, exercising, drinking lots of water, that kind of thing, and that is all very important.

It's very important to stay healthy physically, but what I want to specifically talk about today is good mental health. And certainly you're going to figure out that gratitude is going to be a big part of that.

When you think about taking care of what's going on there and how your mind is influenced, you'll realize the physical factor; doctors tell me that 60-65% of your health and your life is genetic, with maybe a third you can't control yourself. But the whole thing with gratitude is that it conditions the mind every single day to be thinking about everything that is positive in your life, everything that's good in your life, everything that you're grateful for.

Now certainly, some of those things we can't control either, but, just like the physical aspect of health, let's control what we can. I remember years ago I saw a coach on the sideline. He was retiring, a phenomenally successful basketball coach. And the reporter comes up to him with a microphone, and shoves it right in his face, and says, "Listen, coach. You had some 800 odd wins and some 200 or 300 odd loses. How do you feel about the fact you never made it to the final four?"

And the coach looks at him and replies, "Hey, some things just don't work out like we planned." And I thought, that's true, physically, mentally, emotionally, spiritually, financially – all those areas of our life that we pay attention to. But on the mental part, every single day you should focus on gratitude; as you've heard me say many times: if you think about it, it's just a dream; if you talk about it, it inspires; but if you write about it, it empowers you. It truly empowers you when you write those words – "I'm so grateful for this," "I'm so grateful for that."

So remember, to be healthy, stay physically healthy specifically, but really stay healthy mentally as well, and one of the huge, huge components to that, every day, is that gratitude journal. Write all those things you're thankful for on the left-hand side, and all the things you're going to be thankful for on the right-hand side.

Have a grateful day and take care.

27

It Takes As Long As It Takes

I want to talk about your journey, my journey, basically, how we all journey through life. And the concept that I've come to really appreciate, which is that it takes as long as it takes. I think about – I may have mentioned this before – how, when I was 19, I wanted to be a motivational speaker. I always wanted to be in front of people talking about inspiration and positive attitudes and things like that.

It took me almost 40 years to find the message of gratitude. I learned about gratitude, embraced gratitude, embraced the gratitude journal, and I realized along the way that it takes as long as it takes. It's your journey. Don't compare yours to anybody else's. You're a unique person.

We talk a lot about just trying to help you navigate through life. It's going to take as long as it takes. I remember years ago when my son was young. He was trying to play baseball. He had a heck of a time – he couldn't hit, couldn't pitch, couldn't catch, and really couldn't run very fast – but he kept trying.

I remember over and over again, sitting in the stands watching him play, striking out, striking out, running back to the dugout, and sitting in the corner with his face in his hands and just crying. I couldn't go down to the dugout and comfort him. I had to let him stay with the team but I felt terrible just watching. He kept trying and trying and trying.

Eventually, on May 31st, 2005, every parent's dream . . . they're down six to five, two out, two people on base, and my son comes to bat. Ball one, strike one; ball two, strike two; ball three, full count. I'm just sitting there shivering in the stands.

The next pitch, he rips down the third base line. The guy from third comes in. The guy from second rounds third. He heads to home. The ball is late. They win seven to six. My son is on second base. The team runs out, puts him on their shoulders, and carries him off the field.

I had such a lump in my throat, I couldn't talk for probably 20 minutes. But eventually, I collected myself and we talked later that night. I said to him that it was never about baseball. It was about not giving up.

So I think about the long journey I've been on to spread the message about gratitude. It takes as long as it takes. Gratitude is such a huge part of that. Every day, remember to be grateful for everything in your life that is good and wonderful, friends and family, jobs, and all these things that we sometimes take for granted.

Write in that gratitude journal every single day. It will reinforce in your mind everything you're grateful for: today on the left-hand side, everything you're going to be grateful for tomorrow on the right-hand side.

That's it for today. Have a grateful day.

28

Yin and Yang

Okay. Today yin and yang – now what exactly does that mean? It's like a balance. It's like symmetry in life. Common physics and many other aspects of human life will tell you that everything has to have a balance . . . high and low, left and right, good and bad, even up and down.

I thought about this one day: how can you ever really appreciate ups in your life if you haven't experienced downs? You've got to know what it was like down there to know what it's like up here. There's got to be that basis for comparison.

I thought about so many things in life that involved not giving up and this, of course, is where gratitude comes in. How about the salesman? The average number of calls it takes for a salesman to make a sale is four. The average number of calls it takes for a salesman to get discouraged is two. Or about the guy that's digging for that vein of gold? The guy always quits about a foot before the real vein of gold. He's got to hang in there.

And I was thinking about all this balance. What do we want to do with gratitude? We want to tip the scales in our favor. That's what we want to do because there is going to be a balance. There is going to be symmetry. There is going to be left and right and so on. Last night, I was at my son's baseball game. It was a great night for a baseball game, and it was one of these games that went zero-zero. And I thought, "Gosh, is he going to be able to score a run?"

So it finally got to the seventh inning. They still play, of course, seven innings. And as it turned out, there's one or two guys on the bases. My son comes up to bat. He hits a single into the right field. The guy comes around and scores. They're up one to nothing and that's the end of the top of the seventh.

The bottom of the seventh comes up, and there are a couple of guys on base, and then there's an out, and there's another guy on base. Another one is out so it's two outs, the bases are loaded. A big slugger comes up to the mound for the other team, still one to nothing. The batter hits a towering fly ball to centerfield. My son backpedals, backpedals, grabs the ball, and makes the final out. They won the game. I'm ecstatic.

But then I noticed something was sort of strange as I'm walking towards my car. I'm walking towards the parking lot and I thought "What is that on my car?" and I realized "Uh-oh! The foul ball hit the car."

You may be saying, "Well, Brooker, we don't believe you. That's just too easy to use a yin and a yang." Well, here it is. The ball hits squarely above the driver's side of windshield, completely shattered it, and broken glass and shards of glass are over the place.

But there was the yin and yang and I thought that what happened was so phenomenal. I almost believed that it took a shattered windshield for my son to have the winning hit and catch the ball over the final out. It made me feel that great, but it reminded me that there's always this yin and yang, there is always this left and right, there's always this balance.

Well, how can you tip those scales in your favor? Gratitude and specifically, that gratitude journal. Remember, when you're writing in it every single day, you'll focus and reframe and retrain your mind to pay attention to everything you're grateful for, everything you're thankful for, everything you appreciate. It gets your entire mind thinking in terms of tipping that balance in your favor.

So, even like last night, as much as I hated to see

that windshield, I was sure glad to see my son win that game. So make sure you're writing in your gratitude journal every day. If you don't have one, go to http://www.thebrooker.com and you can pick one up.

That's it for now. Have a grateful evening/grateful day. Take care.

29

Father's Day

Today is a very special day for a number of people in this country. It's Father's Day. I'm a father and I wanted to talk about being a father and how gratitude plays a part.

My father passed away many, many years ago but I noticed over the years, as I thought about my father, I wasn't really grateful enough for the things he did for me and for my four siblings. There were five of us growing up. He worked very hard. My mom stayed at home for many, many years while my father went to work. I grew up in the '50s and the '60s, and as I look back on it, really embracing gratitude has really helped me to be much more grateful for the role that my father played, and for how hard he tried to be the best father possible.

Later on in life, I became a father myself. I'm extremely blessed to have two boys; one is 28, one is 18. And as I thought about being a father, I remember having a cup of coffee one day with a good buddy and he said to me "Brooker, I'm going to tell you something. I'm going to tell you the best word you're ever going to hear in the English language."

I remember sitting at this restaurant thinking, "Boy, this is going to be good." But then he said, "Brooker, the best word you're ever going to hear in the English language is the word 'Daddy'." And boy, was he right!

Over the years, as my two sons called me "Daddy," nothing warmed my heart more, and made me feel more proud to be a dad, to be acknowledged as daddy, and the one that is guiding them through life. My 18 year old, the one that had the game which I mentioned, is now taller than I am and occasionally he still slips and calls me "Daddy" – and there's nothing that warms my heart more or melts my heart more than hearing that word from a 6'2" 18-year old and remembering the role that I played.

I've never been prouder of any role I played in my life. It is so wonderful to take somebody who you watched being born as an empty slate and set him the best example possible. And certainly one of those aspects of that is gratitude and I'm trying to teach both my sons, as well as many other people I come in contact with, how powerful gratitude is.

I'm very grateful for my father. I'm extremely grateful for the blessing of being a father myself. No role in my life has been more important to me, and no two people are more important to me on this entire earth than those two sons of mine.

So that's the message for the day. Think about your father a lot. If you're a father yourself, think about being the father that you are. Are you showing that gratitude? Are you being grateful every day? And certainly remember to write in that gratitude journal every single day. At the very bottom on the left-hand side is the Highlight of the Day and when I still occasionally hear that "Daddy" – that becomes my highlight of the day.

So that's it for Father's Day. Don't forget to write in that gratitude journal and have a great Father's Day!

30

Gratitude Intentions

It is the day after Father's Day and I want to talk just about a couple of little interesting things. Number one, we talked before in a previous chapter about being thankful, of course, for friends, and for people that do things for you, and of course being grateful. But today I want to take it a step further. I've had a number of questions about the right-hand side of the gratitude journal, gratitude intentions.

If we look at our journal, you can see that the left-hand side is everything we're grateful for today. Here on the right is everything we're grateful for tomorrow. Well, I think "today" is pretty self-explanatory. I'm very grateful for a phenomenal Father's Day yesterday – the cards I got, some of the text messages, and so forth. And that is everything you're grateful for in the present tense.

On your gratitude intentions everything is all of the things you're going to be grateful for tomorrow and into the future; you should write it as if this actually happened already.

And that is — I'm so grateful for the impact I've had with the message I've delivered about gratitude. I'm so grateful for the phenomenal life that I've had, that my children have had, and so forth. So that is how the right-hand side works. And the brain will actually program itself to see those things as already happening, as they already have, and they're actually in the future. So be thankful for that. Keep in contact with friends, express that gratitude to friends, express things to all those who said "Thank you" or rather "Happy Father's Day," to the fathers who are reading this and so forth.

One more thing on the yin and yang piece in the last chapter . . . I got a couple of messages where people said, "Well, that was great about the baseball game as being the high point of the day and then the smashed windshield kind of balancing things out."

So anyway, that's the message for today. Remember those gratitude intentions. Everything that you're grateful for today is on the left-hand side, and everything you're grateful for on the right is your gratitude intentions, and everything that will happen in the future. And you watch, because those things will happen. I've got many, many examples of my gratitude intentions – of things I am grateful for that hadn't even happened, and sure enough, they happened just as they manifested themselves in my mind.

Have a great day. Talk to you later.

David George Brooke

31

Your Spouse

I was thinking about a couple of days ago about the chapter I did on Father's Day. And I started thinking about gratitude for our parents and our loved ones and people in our lives. So I want to talk specifically about spouses, whether it's a husband, a wife, a boyfriend, a girlfriend, a significant other, whatever term you want to use.

I saw a movie not too long ago and there was kind of a chaotic scene where there is a mother and a father and the children. And apparently the father had done something that wasn't very good, and the mother is very upset with the father, but the daughter is even more upset with the father, and is mad at the mother for not leaving him.

So they had kind of an exchange, the mother and the daughter, and she says, "Mom, why don't you leave Dad? I can't believe he did something like this. How horrible is that?" And she looked back at the daughter and she said, "You know what, I choose to see all the things that are good that he brings to the table that he has done in our marriage, and I choose to look at that and choose not to focus on some of these things that he's done that aren't too good."

So it got me thinking about the whole thing about gratitude when it comes to our spouse. And when you look at your husband or your wife, your boyfriend, your girlfriend, your significant other, it's easy to look at the things that they've not done right, or they don't do this right, or don't do that right, but sometimes, it's really easy to forget all the things that they did that were so good. I don't know why this is – just our need for perfection, or maybe we want to nitpick, or whatever.

So it ties in very nicely to gratitude. Think about your spouse, be very grateful for your spouse, and try to include that in your gratitude journal as well. All those things on the left-hand side are everything we're grateful for today, and everything on the right-hand side is what we're going to be grateful for tomorrow. Think about everything that the spouse does for you.

Think about what your spouse did that day. The highlight of the day certainly could be just their calling to say "I love you" or "I was thinking about you;" that can make your day and increase that daily number.

So spend some time thinking about that, and please put that in the gratitude journal.

Have a grateful day. Write in that gratitude journal. If you need a journal, go to http://www.thebrooker.com. That's it for the day. We'll see you tomorrow.

32

Lookin' Good

Today's subject is called "Lookin' Good." Now what exactly do we mean by looking good? Well, when we think about how we take care of ourselves, we think about how we feel physically, how we feel mentally, how we feel emotionally, spiritually, our family, our careers, and so forth.

I was wondering one day if there is anything more important than your health, being physically fit, because without your health, you really don't have much. So what I'd like you to do today when you're writing your gratitude journal is to prioritize the things that are most important, and start with those first. And certainly being physically healthy is the most important thing.

It's not that you don't have much. Now, some would argue that you want to be mentally healthy too, because you could have a physically fit body but, mentally, be a little bit not right, and that wouldn't be good either. So physically and mentally, both go together and are pretty important. It ties into your emotional relationships with your family and friends and so forth.

So when writing in your gratitude journal, think about being grateful first and foremost for how healthy you are. Then maybe next are family, your spouse (I talked about in the previous lesson), your children (we just talked about Father's Day a few days ago), your friends, your job, your home, any of the things that you know are so great in your life, instead of focusing on those things that are negative.

Now, we also talk about looking good. We talked about being in shape physically, emotionally, financially, spiritually, and so on. With physically, what does that mean? Well, they talk about drinking a lot of water. They talk about exercise. They talk about keeping in contact with your friends, eating right, doing all those things — and let me just add, writing in that daily gratitude journal as well.

Years ago, I had a good friend who always just kept in perfect, perfect shape and just cut. Oh, he looked like kind of a Greek God, if you will. It was always the salad without the dressing, and just a little portion of this, and so forth. One day, I just got frustrated. I looked at him and said, "Can I just ask you something? Wouldn't you like a big piece of chocolate cake, with a bunch of icing on it?"

And he looked at me and he says, "Oh, Dave, Dave, Dave, Dave. I love chocolate cake. It's just that I like looking good just a little bit more." I never forgot that, because it was always about the priorities; chocolate cake was good but looking good was just a little bit more important.

So when you're thinking about looking good, think about how you look physically, mentally, emotionally, financially, spiritually. Think about your family, your career, and so forth. Write in that gratitude journal every single day and try to prioritize it.

Left-hand side for everything you're grateful for today and right-hand side, for everything you're going to be grateful for. But if you prioritize, you always hit the most important things first, and I certainly I think your physical health is more important than anything because without that you don't really have much.

Take care. Bye.

33

The Inmates

Okay. Today's topic: The Inmates. So what is that about? Well, it's interesting. Yesterday, I had the opportunity to speak to about 25, 30 inmates who had just gotten their diplomas for a course from a community college that coordinates with the prisons. And I was struck by a number of things, all of course, revolving around gratitude.

But first and foremost, as I got to meet some of these individuals and listen to some of their stories and so forth, it occurred to me how grateful all of us should be for some of the choices that we made, or didn't make in our lives. In many cases, it so often was the decision to take the left instead of the right, to do something, to stay a little longer with something that gives us a little bit of trouble, something that all of us have experienced.

And I thought back on my life. I thought of all the times that I maybe drove a little faster than I should have, or just took that left turn instead of taking that right turn, or made a decision that could have cost me. Some of these people had been in jail for five years, ten years. Some had been there longer than that. Some had been in solitary confinement.

And as I sat there after speaking and meeting these individuals, I thought about how many choices I have made in my life to put me on the right path instead of the wrong path. And it made me realize how grateful I am for my thought process, for my brain, for the way it works, that made me make some choices that turned out better instead of worse.

The other big thing that really hit me was, when you looked at these individuals, you saw a cross-section of life at age 25 or 30. Maybe eight or ten were women, young, old, black, white, heavy, thin, tall, short. It could have been a group of 25 or 30 people walking through your local mall. That's how diverse they were and that's how interesting it is that you don't have a stereotype – "Oh, this is a person that went to jail" – all sorts of reasons, but always coming back to being grateful for the choices that you made.

So really think about that when you're talking and thinking about your gratitude every single day and especially when you're writing in your gratitude journal – how grateful you are for all those choices you made, good choices when sometimes "just that close," can be the difference between going down the right road and going down the wrong road.

So that's it for today. Have a grateful day.

34

Stick With It

Today's topic is Stick with It. Now, what do I mean by "stick with it"? I was thinking about something yesterday. I had just wrapped up a problem I've had for a long time. Gosh, I would say the solution to this problem was maybe a dozen years in the making, but I stuck with it and never gave up on it. I would make it akin to running a marathon. I ran one marathon a long time ago. I used to talk about breaking it down into bite-size pieces, but the biggest thing was to stick with it.

And I started thinking about all life's challenges. Gratitude is such a great piece to add into your life, being grateful for some of the things that happened to you. Be grateful for the fact that you had problems and you can solve the problems by sticking with it.

There are so many great analogies, so many great values, that will come out of sticking with something, and seeing the problems on the other side as you look back on it. Think about push-ups;

they say the push-ups 22, 23, 24, 25 are easier for you than the first 21 because you just stuck with it and built that muscle along the way.

My mom had a great saying. In fact, she had two great sayings (well, many great sayings but two that really stuck out to me). Once, she looked at me and asked, "David, where does it say life is easy?" "Gosh, I don't know, mom."

She was really like a bulletin board. She used to say some words like a road sign. And she'd also say, "Where does it say life is fair?" And the answer is life is neither easy nor fair, but it's just the way it is.

But we've got to be grateful, although we have problems, because when you think about it — when you really think about it — you should be grateful you have problems because without problems in life, what would you have? And I think kind of the whole goal is to have better problems, better quality problems.

It's like when you're younger and you don't maybe have as many resources, you're not really sure what you're going to be able to spend on something, and you may have to choose the least expensive option. But as you get older, you get to choose between A and B. The fact that you get to choose makes that a better quality problem.

Be really glad that happens to you, because in so many ways, that's how we process things – a piece at a time, sticking with it, going all the way through, making sure that you know at some point you're going to see that end in sight. And when you reach that end and you look back, it's never as bad as when you were thinking about it.

It's like waking up in the middle of the night – I don't know if this ever happens to you – you wake up and all these problems are scrambling around in your head, and it seems like it's overwhelming. A few times along the way, I've gotten up, and written them all down – they never looked as bad on a piece of paper as they did rolling around in my head. So stick with it, piece by piece.

Remember to be grateful that you got problems in your life, especially better quality problems, because problems will always be there. It's like that first sentence in that book – "Life is difficult." It *is* difficult, but at least if you have better quality problems, you're going to have an excellent life figuring out this way, and being very satisfied that you got over those hurdles. So stick with it. I just remembered this recently, on my deal of 12 to 13 years to resolve that problem. It's behind me now.

So that's it for the day. Be grateful. Be grateful for your health. Be grateful that you've got problems to solve.

35

Don't Do It Halfway

Okay, today's subject: Don't do it halfway. Now what do I mean by that? Of course, we're talking about gratitude. Don't make a half-baked effort at gratitude. Fully embrace gratitude, fully embrace a gratitude journal, and you will see how it will change your life.

I mentioned before about how I worked for a large retailer that was very proud of the way they presented their products. A very, very successful retailer – a Fortune 50 company. And they used to always say, "Do it right or don't do it at all." So, translation – don't do it halfway. You know you've heard many times that, "You never get a second chance to make a first impression." Well, I've also heard, "You never get a second chance to do it right the first time."

So when you're approaching gratitude, make really sure that you fully embrace it. You will not believe how it will manifest itself in your life, and the things that will start happening because of your being grateful for everything around you, and recording it every day in your gratitude journal.

 I remember hearing a story once that I thought was kind of interesting in terms of how we decide, which direction we seem to go, wanting to do it halfway or what have you. A cop saw a guy speeding and running a stop sign. He pulls him over, the lights are flashing and everything. He goes up and talks to the guy in the car and says, "You didn't come to a full stop."

The guy answers, "Yes, I did."

The cop disagrees, saying "No, you didn't. You didn't come to a full stop."

The driver says, "Well, I kind of slowed down. What's the difference?"

The cop goes, "Step out of the car."

The guy steps out of the car. The cop takes out his nightstick, starts beating on the guy and the guy says, "Ow, ow, ow!"

He's hitting him all over the head and the guy yells, "What are you doing?"

The cop says, "Well, let me ask you something; do you want me to slow down or do you want me to stop? What's the difference?"

So the point is, make sure you fully embrace it. Don't do it halfway. Think about it. Every single day, prioritize the things that are most important in your life: your health, your family, the roof over your head, your friends, the job, all the things you have to be thankful for. It'll continue to bubble up inside you and will continue to manifest itself and really, really good things will happen to your life.

And remember, everything you're grateful for will be on the left hand side, everything you're going to be grateful for on the right hand side.

So don't do it halfway. Embrace it fully and be grateful. Believe me; it will pay huge dividends — you can't even imagine.

Have a great day and we'll see you tomorrow. Take care.

David George Brooke

36

Always Hang in There

Okay, today, I have kind of a special message. Although I want to make sure that you think about gratitude and how it affects your life, we also need to think about something else that's big. Always, always, always hang in there. Never give up.

You can tell that's kind of a theme that I go through quite a bit. Don't ever give up. Hang in there. Don't do it halfway. Always stay to the finish. Go through the entire process. How many times have you left a problem behind, and it's still sitting out there waiting for you? But if you stuck with it, and finished it, completed that marathon, whatever it might be, you got great satisfaction. There was a tremendous feeling, when it was completed and you could look at the lessons you learned.

Today, I want to give an example of why you always want to hang in there. My son was four and a half years old when my wife, his mother, died; my older son was 14. Then, within six months of my wife's death, I was told that my younger son was way behind in school.

And I remember very clearly going in and listening to these counselors go over what they had put him through, this fine-motor and gross-motor and all these skill sets and at the end of the day, they finally come to me and say, "He's way behind. You're going to have to hold him back. He doesn't get it." He's got major difficulties, a learning disorder, you name it.

I was crushed because I couldn't say anything. Gosh, he'd just lost his mother, but what I never forgot is what the lady said to me just as I was about to leave. I had said, "Well, you know, he's going to be the quarterback when he's in high school."

She goes, "He's not going to be any quarterback in any team, any time soon. I wouldn't even count on that for a second."

I remember thinking, "Wow! What a great positive way to send off something to a father about their child."

Well, as time went on, my son did have a difficult time in school and in sports, but then he started to get it and he got better and better and better, and he just hung in there along the way.

I've told you before about the baseball game (but

now, I'm so proud, I'm telling it again in this new context), and how I remember one day when he was about 13 years old, going to this baseball game and it was every parent's nightmare, where he'd gone constantly to the dugout and cried and couldn't catch and couldn't run and couldn't hit, couldn't field, and it was just really, really painful to watch him.

But eventually that game was in the bottom of the seventh inning, two out, boys on second and third, and my son comes to bat. It worked to a full count and the next pitch; he rips it down the third baseline just inside the bag. The guy from third comes in. The guy from second runs for third, heading for home. The ball is late; he slides under the tag. They win the game eight to seven. My son's on second base, and the team carries him off on his shoulders.

And I remember that I couldn't even talk for about two or three minutes; I had such a gigantic lump in my throat. But when we got home, he and I sat down and I said, "You know, it was never about baseball. It was about the fact you hung in there. It was about you never gave up. You went through the tears, you went through all the frustration, but you kept trying."

So remember, be grateful for having the ability to try to hang in there, to never give up, to never stop.

Take it in bite-size pieces, I said in an earlier chapter. Break it down into something you can handle. Running the marathon, I ran 26 miles, and I just thought about a mile or two at a time.

Be grateful for all the skills that you have inside you that will deliver you these end results, even when it seems pretty challenging. I know my son sure is; now he's the starting pitcher on the baseball team. So it's been a great, great story to illustrate why you got to just hang in there.

You write in that gratitude journal every single day. I promise you, it'll manifest itself in a way you can't even imagine. All right, you take care. We'll see you tomorrow.

37

This Too Shall Pass

Okay, so for today, I started thinking, how do we handle things when things happen that upset us? Things that get under our skin, traumatic things, small things, big things, whatever. Well, I had a good example a couple of days ago.

I'm always talking about a gratitude journal. I'm always talking about my gratitude journal – The Brooker's daily gratitude journal. Every single day, recording the highlights of your day, special events. Everything you're grateful for today on the right hand side, everything that you're going to be grateful for tomorrow on the left hand side, and at the bottom, the highlight of your day.

Well, sadly, this past weekend, I lost my gratitude journal. I'd gone to my son's baseball tournament, and tried to retrace my steps, and I'll be darned if I know what happened to it. I may have put it on top of the car and it may have fallen off or something, but I was very upset as I've had gratitude journals last about three months, about 90 days, and I was probably halfway into this one – a lot of really good, good entries, including what one of my sons did for Father's Day. Some of the really neat things and some of those really cool highlights and most importantly of all, what I was grateful for every single day as well as records of my daily number.

But then I thought about that great passage: "This too shall pass." And I think of that passage when we really think about how we deal with traumatic events, things that are upsetting. This really bothered me because, again, there was about a month and a half worth of entries in there. Well, there wasn't much I was going to be able to do about it. I kind of brought it back into focus.

I'm grateful for the fact that I have this gratitude journal every single day. I grabbed a new blank book and started fresh a couple of days ago, when I realized I wasn't going to find the old one, and I started moving forward again.

So think about how we deal with things when things are upsetting to us. How do we process them? How do we actually see again the good and bad in everything that happens to us, and most of all, remember, "this too shall pass." I'm off to a good start on my next journal and that's just the way it goes.

So that's it for the day. Remember to be writing in that gratitude journal every single day, record it — on the left hand side what you're grateful for today, and on the right hand side what you're grateful for tomorrow.

Have a grateful day and remember: "this too shall pass" as does everything that happens to your life that occasionally throws you a curve. Take care.

38

4th of July

Okay, the 4th of July. We're celebrating that holiday today and I was thinking about the 4th of July and what it really represented. And yes, of course it's called the 4th of July but it is, in fact, Independence Day – independence for our country. But how about independence for you and me? How about having the freedom to make our own choices, and the perspective that freedom gives us?

I spoke in a previous chapter about talking to a group of inmates and the strong impact it had on me. I've been so grateful for my freedom. How grateful are we for the men and women that fight for this country to make sure that we are free? Something, again, that is so critical, and we need to stop and think about it, and really, really be grateful about it.

I also thought it's always about perspective – how we look at things. As you look at those fireworks bursting up in the air, yes, they're great, and they're colorful, and they're exciting, but they really represent that freedom and that independence in a big way.

Every year, on the 4th of July, we watch those fireworks. They represent all those people who have come before us to give us the free land that we live in, and our free will, as much as anything. We get to choose whatever we want to do.

But I thought about perspective, too, for a second. I thought about this – it's always how we look at things. I remember the story about the two candy stores on each side of the street. And how each sold an ounce of candy for five cents.

One day, the owner of one of the stores was looking through the window – all of the kids in the town went to the store across the street and he couldn't figure it out. Same price, five cents for an ounce, same candy, fresh, good. He had available the most popular and the most current candies, but why did all the kids go over there?

So he pulled a little boy aside one day to ask him a question. And he said, "The same things, we have the same candy, the same things," and so on and so forth. "Why do you go into my competitor across the street instead of coming to me?"

And the boy answered, "Well, when we came to your store, you poured a bunch of candy onto the scale, and then you started scooping away, scooping away, scooping away, to finally get down to an ounce. But Mr. Smith on the other side of the street, he pours a little candy and adds more, adds more, adds more, adds more, gets up to that ounce."

And that's why all those kids went there, because it was a completely different perspective – taking away all the candy after dumping it all in or starting with a little bit and adding, and adding, and adding to come up to that ounce. So it's always about perspectives.

So think about that on this 4th of July. Think about how grateful we are. Think about the independence that we enjoy as a people, as a nation, and think about it when you write in your gratitude journal. Don't forget that gratitude journal.

That's it for the day. Have a great 4th of July. We'll see you tomorrow.

David George Brooke

39

Heart Attack!

Okay, today – heart attack. That is the title of today's chapter. What's that about? Well, I just got back from the hospital. A very close friend of mine who I've known for over 40 years had a heart attack on Saturday. It actually looked quite serious. In fact, on Saturday, I wasn't sure how he was going to do. I stopped by the hospital and he literally looked lifeless. Well, I just got back a little bit ago and he looks a lot better.

Once again, it brought me back to this whole subject of gratitude and being grateful for our help. When we talk about our daily gratitude journal, one of the biggest things we talk about, if not the biggest, is our health. I think that without your health, you don't have anything else. And I've mentioned that if you've got your health, your family, and your friends, and activities, and things like this, you're to be grateful. And to have a roof over your head and a bed to sleep in and so forth.

But I think what's interesting is, once again, this is an individual friend of mine, as I said, who I've known for over 40 years, picture of health, works out, always had a great attitude, doesn't smoke, doesn't drink, takes really good care of himself and Boom – just like that, I could have lost him, and that is how fast it could happen.

So remember, be grateful for your health and take care of yourself. Remember, the physical being is just as important as the mental part and part of that mental aspect is that gratitude journal; when you're programming your mind to be grateful for everything in your life, it is positive.

I talked a lot recently about all of your positive qualities. Focus on those. Don't worry about the negative things. Don't worry about the things you're not as good at; focus on all the things, those positive qualities, you have. Be grateful for your health; be grateful for your friends; be grateful for your family and be grateful for all of those other things in your life that you have that are so good.

So remember, take care of yourself. Write in that gratitude journal every single day and be grateful. We'll see you tomorrow.

40

We Want You to Be The Jury Foreman

Today, what I want to talk about is embracing and being grateful for the qualities that you have – whether they be leadership, organizing activities, teaching, being an artistic person, whatever they are. I want you to remember to be grateful for those talents that you have, because many of those are God-given. Some we create ourselves but I think a lot of them are God-given.

And I think about my case; one of my God-given talents is being a leader. I always had been the guy that's kind of at the front of the group, organizing and leading things.

I think back years ago when I had an experience that really illustrated it for me. I was called to jury duty and I went to the jury pool, and waited a few days to get onto this case, and so forth. The case was an assault with a deadly weapon.

And so we listened to the testimony for three or four days and, although I'd never been on a jury before, it was quite a good experience, and I highly recommend it for those of you who have not had that opportunity. But the case wrapped up, the prosecutor made his closing arguments, and the defense made his, so we went into the jury room.

Now mind you, we'd not spoken a word to each other in the four, five days. We're not supposed to talk at all. I was dressed very casually, just in jeans and a sweatshirt so there was nothing that would indicate at all, really, what we did for a living, or what have you. But the twelve of us go into the room, the bailiff comes in, and he says, "Okay, a couple of things. The first thing we want you to do is elect a jury foreman, and then, if you need any evidence to be brought into the jury room, let us know. I'll check back in about an hour to see if you have any questions."

Everybody looks at him, "Okay, great." He goes out and closes the door.

Ten of the 11 people point to me and say, "We want you to be the jury foreman." I kind of laughed and thought "What is it with me just having this natural tendency to be the leader?" So I popped up, grabbed a felt tip pen, wrote my name down, David Brooke, and "What's your name," and went around and took an initial vote on what we all thought of this person that was suspected of assault with a deadly weapon.

So my point is, embrace and be grateful for the talents that you have, and make the most of them. And make your strengths productive and your weaknesses irrelevant. And I think it's something as an example for me, that I always realized that I'm supposed to be the leader; I'm supposed to be the jury foreman; I'm supposed to be the pilot of the plane; I'm supposed to drive the hydroplane. Whatever it might be, it's just something that's been part of my DNA since I was small.

So embrace that gratitude and remember to really, really feel good about the strengths that you have, and make the most of them.

That's it for now. Have a grateful day. Take care.

41

Stand By Your Principles

Okay, today I want to talk about, naturally, gratitude as usual, but I also want to talk about standing by your principles. And by that, I mean, I want you to think about all the things that you are grateful for that have to do with the fact that you stood by your principles, stood by your word, stood up for yourself, or just in general, chose to tell people, "I'm going to stand for this and this is what I mean by what I say," and didn't back down.

I think about many instances in my life when somebody had to make me make a stand. And I thought, "I'm grateful for the fact that I've got this attitude that I'm going to believe in what I say, back it up and not let anybody affect overall how I think about something by just agreeing with whoever is in the room at the time."

I think back to years ago when I was a freshman in college. My folks had gotten divorced and as part of the divorce settlement, my father was to pay for my college and that of my older brother and I think a couple of my younger brothers as well.

So during the first year of having him pay for it, I constantly heard about how hard it was on him. Even though he was a very successful attorney, I heard about how hard it was for him to be paying my college tuition as well as my room and board in a fraternity and so forth.

So I listened to it for about a year. I came into the start of my sophomore year and he was supposed to pay for all four years. And I'd heard for the entire first year about how much of a struggle it was for him and, in fact, I'll never forget he even said that he and his wife had to subsist on macaroni and cheese because David was costing them so much money.

So I remember the start of my sophomore year, I walked in his office and he said, "Well, here's the check for your first quarter and once again, we're barely making it, we're really struggling."

I remember the moment that was going to define me for the rest of my life because I was going to stand by my principles and I was going to be grateful that I had principles in my life. I took the check, tore it into literally several hundred pieces, tossed them on the desk and I said, "You will never pay for another cent of my college again."

I actually got quite emotional about it and he just looked at me and I turned around and walked out of the office. And I realized right then that I was going to have to pay for the rest of my college myself and I did just that. My sophomore year, my junior year, my senior year, and then I graduated and got my bachelor's degree.

But as I look back on it, I was so proud of myself for standing by that principle and being grateful that I had a principle to embrace. I also think the extra bonus to the whole thing was that I actually ended up appreciating my college degree even more because I paid for it myself.

It was tough because I had to work fulltime and was also taking a full load of classes. But in the long run, I was very, very grateful for upholding that principle.

So think about the principles that you represent, think about the ones that you embrace, and be sure to stand by them. You will be very grateful in the long run. That's it for the day. Have a grateful day and we'll see you tomorrow. Take care.

David George Brooke

42

Learn to Listen

Okay, today I want to do something a little bit different. Certainly, I always want to talk about gratitude. But I want to talk about something that will make you even more grateful and certainly make your friends and family and the other people around you grateful and that's the ability to listen.

It's so important to listen. I believe it was once said that the Lord gave us one mouth and two ears and we should use them in that proportion. But I realize too that we're in such a fast-paced world now that people don't always pay attention. So be grateful for having those two ears and just one mouth, and use them in proportion, as they say.

I remember a little story about two guys on an airplane. They boarded the plane in Los Angeles and flew to New York and it was like six hours in the plane. One guy talked the entire way. They landed in New York, got off the plane and their wives picked them up. And the wife of the gentleman that talked the entire way asks him, "How was your flight?" and he says, "I met the nicest guy on the airplane."

So remember when you listen that, like anything else, you're going to learn so much more about somebody else, if you really pay close attention to him, make eye contact, and be grateful that you have that friend or other person whose story you get to hear. However, like so many other things in life, it's always about moderation. I've had many conversations with people in which I've said or they've said to me, "Okay, enough about me. Let's talk about you." Keep the balance.

I remember years ago, I was dating a young lady and I was a very good listener, really paying attention and asking a lot of questions. I was very proud of myself because I really listened very intently. And again, I was grateful to have a date and maybe have a new friend. So as we get to the end of the date, we're walking to the car, and I say, "I think we should go out again."

And she goes, "I don't think so." I went "Really?" I was kind of taken aback because I thought we had a good time and again, I had listened very carefully.

And I say, "Well, gosh, may I ask why?" and she goes, "I don't know if that was a date or more of an interrogation." And I realized you've got to have a balance. Ask questions, talk, listen, have the balance, have moderation.

Be grateful for the friends you have. Listen to their stories. Pay attention to what they're saying; give them some input when they ask for it, but really pay attention and listen carefully. It will return itself in spades and believe me, you'll notice a big difference. So be grateful for those beautiful friends. Be grateful for that ability to listen and most of all, just be grateful for all the qualities that you have and you bring to the table for that friendship with those friends, family, people you work with, what have you.

Thanks a lot. We'll see you tomorrow.

43

Don't Compare Yourself to Anyone Else

Okay, today I want to talk about being grateful for who you are. And I want you to think back. I've mentioned this when I've talked about the kind of person you are and the qualities you bring to the table and I was thinking one of the things that somebody told me years ago: don't ever compare yourself to anybody else.

Many times in my life, I've thought that you want to achieve big goals, you want to try to be the best you can, but you should always remember to be the best that you can be and not worry so much about somebody else. I remember years ago when I ran a lot of 10Ks and eventually ran a marathon. When I was running in one of these races, there was one that was across a floating bridge. It's about two miles longer so you could kind of see the entire group of the runners.

Anyway, it was a rainy day. It was really a tough run, little kids are passing me, I don't feel good, and the rains are coming down and so forth. I looked in front of me and I just see tons and tons of runners. And you know how when you run along, it's kind of hard to look behind yourself because you already kind of moving forward. But I managed to turn my head and I saw thousands of runners behind me.

And it occurred to me that very moment: "Wow, if all of these people in front of me weren't here, I'd be in first place." So it depends on how you look at it. But don't compare yourself to anybody else.

And so that's the message to remember. Always try to achieve the goals that you set for yourself but don't compare yourself to anybody else. Everybody is unique; keep shooting for the top and you'll always improve yourself. Use those people as role models. But remember, we all have unique strengths and abilities that we bring to the table.

So remember that for today. We'll see you tomorrow. Again, go to http://www.thebrooker.com if you need a gratitude journal. Write in that gratitude journal every single day. I promise you it will make a huge difference. We'll see you tomorrow.

44

Say Thank You

Okay, today I want to talk about saying "Thank you." When you think about gratitude, you think about expressing your feelings, your appreciation, your thankfulness for situations, for your life, for your health, for people, and so forth. But I want to talk in particular today about saying "Thank you" to those people who are around you.

Now, you're thinking in this crazy world we live in, there are so many more ways of showing your appreciation. You can tweet something. You can e-mail a friend. You can post it on Facebook. You can send them a voice mail. There are all these different ways. Or even send an old-fashioned little thing called the letter. There's even a thing that we used years ago called the postcard.

There's also a company called SendOutCards. It does a great job if you go online and maybe send out a card to a person. But we think about how much we want to say thank you, and think about the times people have showed their gratitude towards you, their appreciation, their thankfulness, their thanks, and how that made you feel.

Many times, when I give talks, people tell me that I've just changed their lives with some of the things I've said. They show tremendous gratitude for some of the stories, for some of the techniques I told them that they could utilize to help get through this world, the gratitude journal, and so forth. It makes me feel phenomenal inside. So think about that. Say "Thank you." Say it a lot and show your appreciation.

And remember too, when someone gives you a compliment, that there's a right and a wrong way to take a compliment. If somebody says, "Boy, that sure is a nice sweater," what do a lot of people say? "What, this old rag? I just picked it up at the dump."

My mother once told me there are two ways to accept a compliment, two ways and two ways only: "Thank you," is number one and "Thank you. It's nice of you to say that," is number two. So remember that, even when things go sideways.

I had a friend some years ago that showed me there are always things that can get you back on track. We had some harsh words. I didn't speak to him for several years. All of a sudden one day, he calls me and says, "I'd like to ask for your forgiveness." I never forgot the way it was said, it was so powerful. And I said, "You bet."

We chatted a little bit, got back on track, and I just admired so much his ability to call me. I was so grateful to him for having the courage to call me, apologize, and move forward. So remember to say thank you . . . verbally, text, written, cards, you name it. Believe me, it will make a huge difference.

45

Work Ethic

Okay, today's topic is Work Ethic. Now here's the thing about a work ethic: I think you either get it or you don't. I think you either have it or you don't. I'm just not so sure that you can say, "Well, I'm so grateful. I need a work ethic. I'm going to go take a class, Work Ethic 101, pass the class and all of a sudden, I'll get it."

And I think the reason that I want to bring it up is for gratitude's sake, because you've got to realize that life is going to have these ups and downs. I've certainly had my share; I've talked about a lot of them and have also explained how I've had to bounce back from a lot of adversity.

I remember earlier in my 20s, I had invested in a bunch of property and made quite a bit of money. I learned how to fly. I bought an airplane. I got a fancy car. I was flying high, literally and figuratively.

And then, by my mid-30s, it all kind of came crashing down. I lost everything and gosh, it was, I think five or ten years later, not only had I lost everything, but I had to stay with a friend with my young son.

And I remember one night, lying in the sleeping bag, cuddling my young son, looking skyward, going insane and saying silently to myself, "So it's come to this." Everything was gone, all the material possessions. I still had my health. I still had my son, actually my two sons.

But everything else was gone, and I started thinking right then: so, are you even able to battle back from this and do you even have the same work ethic that got you there in the first place, making all that money, and being successful. And being somebody who you knew could start at the bottom of the mountain and make it to the top? It was all about work ethic.

So I've talked about this a lot lately. Be grateful for the attributes that you have. Be grateful for the talents and the skills and the positives. Forget about the negatives.

Make your strengths productive; make your weaknesses irrelevant because they truly are. But it was my work ethic that got me back again to spread this message of gratitude, being back on top of my game after bouncing back from some of the lowest points in my life, times I couldn't imagine ever having to go through.

Think about your work ethic. Think about what you're grateful for. Think about all those positive attributes. And remember; be writing in that gratitude journal every single day. When you write it down, it activates your reticular activating system and plants it in your brain.

That's it for the day. Be grateful. We'll see you tomorrow.

46

Your Job

Okay, today I want to talk about your job. I was thinking about this today as I went in and out of appointments and talked to various people who were employers, employees; some are the owners, some are the workers. It didn't really matter. And I thought "What is it about people? They don't appreciate their job." How about being grateful for your job?

I remember reading an article years ago, words to the effect of — the ten reasons that people work. It had nothing to do with compensation, the pay that you get. It was camaraderie, and it was making friends, and having a sense of accomplishment, and a sense of being a part of the team. And as I mentioned, there were probably a total of ten different reasons, why people work for jobs and have jobs, that had nothing to do with the pay.

Certainly, today, the cost of benefits are a huge thing. There are a lot of people, who, if it weren't for the cost of medical and other benefits, the advantages of a 401K and so forth, wouldn't really care as much about the wage or salary or what have you. But once again, I go back to being grateful.

We have a lot of unemployment in the country, 8, 9, 10, 11, 12%, depending on the area, and I think about this every day, when I'm writing in that gratitude journal about how grateful I am to have a job, how grateful I am to get that paycheck every other Friday. You don't have to worry about taking care of the bills – you've got money coming in – medical, dental, vision, 401K, whatever it might be.

So we really stop and think about that. I also read a survey some years ago that said 60-70% of the people in this country hated their jobs. "Hate" is a word that I try not even to have in my vocabulary but that is exactly the word that they used in the survey –they *hate* their jobs. How sad is that? And why has it happened that Monday is the worst day of the week, Friday's the best, Wednesday is hump day, and so forth?

So think about that, but not just that when you're writing in your gratitude journal. Think about how grateful you are to have a job, to work for a good company, and if you don't, maybe you're just that much closer to getting the job, if you keep going out there and trying.

But remember, it is always about gratitude,

appreciation, and thankfulness, seeing that glass as half full. So be grateful for that job, take a look around tomorrow or the next day or on Monday when you're at your job again. Think about how much you really appreciate it.

Have a great day and have a grateful day. See you.

47

The Golf Tournament

Okay, the Golf Tournament – what's that about? How does that relate to gratitude? Well, yesterday, I went to a golf tournament that was put on by a couple of really neat guys that I went to high school with. They've done this, I think six or seven years in a row. But they've also been the people who have always tried on a regular basis throughout the year to keep people from high school connected. I graduated with about 500, 550 people. I think close to 15-20% of them have already passed on.

So as I was at the golf tournament yesterday, I was thinking the golf was fun and it was neat to be out in the sun, get a little color, and actually do some golfing, and have some fun. But you know what, the big thing was the connection with all the people – the stories, seeing how people are doing – and this is something I noticed that was really interesting. If you think back about your high school experience or earlier days, the people that got together are these group of friends, the cliques, whatever you want to call them.

I noticed over time, that's all fallen away, and people are just so happy to see you – happy to see you alive, happy to see you happy. And I've also noticed this at reunions, which I highly encourage you to attend when you can, golf tournaments, get-togethers, mid-year things, whatever it might be. I highly encourage you to attend those things. It's so neat because anything that somebody felt back in high school is all gone away.

It's all about, "Are you healthy, how is the wife — or the husband or the kids, —how's things going, what you have been up to?" And it's really, really neat to see this real sense of camaraderie. And I think more than anything else, and the reason I'm bringing it up today, is being grateful for having friends. The most important thing you need to have in your life is your health, next is your family and friends, and other things that happen to you.

I've come across people from time to time that don't have any friends and I just feel bad for them because it's a very reciprocal type of deal; you've got to keep the phone calls and the messages going back and forth to keep those friendships alive.

As we get older, sometimes that's one of the best things we can hang on to; add a phenomenal time and it's just great. I didn't think much about the golf or the good or the bad shot but I sure thought about some of those conversations, talking to these people who were listening to me, to these old friends or people that I had been a friend with for 30, 40, almost 50 years.

Gosh, it was fantastic. I highly recommend that you stay connected. It will really, really enhance your life as you go forward. It's another one of many things you will find you will be grateful for.

So that's it for today. Have a great day. By the way, be writing in that gratitude journal every day. If you don't have one, go to http://www.thebrooker.com and pick one up. Again, it will transform your life and it will get that brain thinking about everything you're grateful for, every single day. Have a grateful day.

48

I Wanna Be A Blue Angel

Okay, for today's discussion around gratitude, I want you to go back a few years. Depending on how old you are, this might be a few years; it might be a lot of years. In my case, it's actually a lot of years.

What did you want to be when you grew up? That is one of the classic questions that was asked all through kindergarten, grade school and so on and so forth. "Hey, what do you want to be when you grow up?" Maybe even going into junior high and high school, who knows when?

But long ago when I was in my early twenties. I made a list of the top 100 things I wanted to do before I left this earth. I know later on that was called a bucket list or what have you; in fact, I'm not even sure where the term *bucket list* came from. I know there was a movie called that. Perhaps it was the things you wanted to do before you kicked the bucket. That is kind of a negative way of looking at it. But nonetheless, I always had my top 100 list.

One of the things I wanted was to be a Blue Angel. I had everything. I wanted to learn how to fly. I wanted to jump out of an airplane. I wanted to climb a mountain. There were all sorts of things, and as I'd seen uncles and aunts and grandparents pass on, and later on, a lot of people in my personal life who were a lot closer to me and a lot younger, it made it even more important for me to take advantage of this top 100 list.

Well, this week, during the annual celebration that we have in the city, the Blue Angels are here. In fact, I may get out tomorrow and take a look at them. I've seen them many, many times. But I want you to remember to be grateful for being healthy. I've talked about this a lot lately, being grateful for all the attributes that you have, the things that you bring to the table, all of your strengths.

Don't worry about your weaknesses. But also remember that I wanted to be a Blue Angel. It's a little bit late now. So I strongly encourage you to put together a top 20 list, top 50, top 100, whatever things you want to do later in life and before you pass on. But remember, there are certain things that can only happen at a certain age at a certain time. There are a lot of things I want to do, now that I realize it's not all that much fun getting older. But remember that you do get a lot smarter, and that is one of the biggest things. A lot wiser, some of the things that really make a difference.

So when I think about wanting to be a Blue Angel, that was great, but that was back then. Now I have to have a different set of targeted things that work for my age, or my skill set, or my physical abilities, which in my case, knock on wood, are still good.

So keep that in mind, make that list. Be grateful that you're thinking about those things. Some people don't think much past about five minutes from now. Be thinking about a year from now, five, and ten, and so forth. Make that list. Be grateful for it. Keep it close to you and refer to it from time to time. It will pay off.

Have a grateful day. Enjoy the day. We'll see you.

49

Who Influences You?

Okay, today – who influences you? I want to talk about this and, of course, I want to talk about how it relates to being grateful. But I want you to think today about how you decide who you let influence you. I think about years ago. I was actually in first grade. I will never forget this story. I met a girl and of course, we're both 6 years old. Her name was Allison and gosh, I guess I better not say her last name, because I have to protect the innocent, even though it was like over 50 years ago.

But I remember just thinking that everything was cool, and we hooked up, and we were out on the monkey bars and in the sandbox and everything, and I said, "I think we should get married."

She looks at me and says, "David, we're six years old. I think we have a whole life in front of us. I think we need to reconsider. You need to reconsider more specifically."

Of course, I laughed and it made me think way back when you're in kindergarten, first grade and on forward, who do you let influence you in your life, and who do you listen to?

One of the things I've said many times is to always consider the source of what you listen to and who you let affect your life. I've been through a lot in my life. I talk about that in many of the videos and talks that I do and one of the things I talk about is how gratitude has transformed me, refocused, reframed my life as one of very, very positive attributes and in looking at things from a positive side.

I've said many times if you want to learn how to swim, ask Michael Phelps. So always think about who is influencing you in your life. It doesn't mean they can't be good friends, or close friends, or acquaintances, or whatever it might be, but always consider the source.

For about six or seven years, I had my own business and unfortunately, at the end of those years, my wife passed away. I just couldn't hang on to the business, so I ended up closing it. It was a very sad and stressful time for me.

But during that time, I remember how many times I'd hear a sentence that started with these two words, "You should." "You should do this with your business, you should open a business here, you should carry this, you should not carry that" and of course, I always wanted to sarcastically say, "And I'm sorry. How is that working for you? Wait a second . . . you don't have your own business."

I know people were trying to be helpful. I know they wanted to give me suggestions, but it made me again think about who I listen to, and who influences me. So think about today; who influences you? Think about their background. Are they positive, are they negative, are they up or are they down? Are they using gratitude in their life? Maybe they are even writing in a gratitude journal?

I talk all the time about how much writing in a gratitude journal can absolutely enhance your life, because you're writing it down, not just thinking and talking about it, but writing down everything that you're grateful for.

So think about that for today. Think about it over the next few days. Who influences you, and who do you let determine the direction that you want to go? Be writing in that gratitude journal every day. If you need one go to http://www.thebrooker.com It's right there on the screen. Have a grateful day. We'll talk to you tomorrow.

David George Brooke

50

Your Children

All right, today: your children. As with most topics that come up when I talk about gratitude, what does that mean? Well, some of you out there have children, some of you don't, but I will guarantee that all of you interact with people in your life, whether it's your children, whether you manage employees, or around your friends, or around your family, or anybody in your social network and those people are watching you. Certainly, your children are probably the best example of all.

So think about how you are setting that example . . . again, whether it's gratitude, the way you follow through, the way you act, the way you listen, all those types of things.

The thing that I learned over all of these years is that, especially children, but anybody in those groups I mentioned earlier, are people who watch what you do. You can talk about, "I'm going to smoke but I don't want you to smoke," or, "I'm not going to exercise but I want you to exercise," and that is fine, but that is not going to be an effective way to lead people or to raise children.

So the same thing is true with gratitude, which is why I always bring it back to everything that you're grateful for, and are you setting a good example for your children? For your friends, for your employees, for your family? — whoever it might be that you're interacting with on a regular basis.

My boys are 28 and 18 now. I think the roles change, but when they were young, hopefully, I set the best example possible, even through a lot of the traumatic events that happened to me along the way. But now, they're older. I heard a friend say this recently, and it was just a great comment. He said, "You know what? You're not going to be involved in their lives quite as much, but be there when they need you."

And I think part of that is setting that example from early on, about how gratitude is a part of my life, how appreciation is a part of my life. Just remember that is how people are going to look at you, and they are going to watch what you do, and not what you say. So be writing in that gratitude journal. Be grateful every day. Show your appreciation. Send a card, send a text, and send an email. Remember every day to express gratitude to somebody who is in your life. It will come back to you tenfold.

So that is the message for today. Remember, if you do need a gratitude journal you can get it at http://www.thebrooker.com

That is it for the day. Have a grateful day. Keep writing in that journal. Take care.

About The Author

David George Brooke

The Brooker – That Gratitude Guy

As a sought after speaker at Rotaries, Chambers, schools, and businesses, David Brooke delivers a message of hope through the power of living a life with gratitude.

The author of "The Brooker's Daily Gratitude Journal" and a co-author of the Amazon Best Seller, "The Gratitude Book Project", David specializes in coaching people to overcome any obstacle through the power of gratitude, specifically through the use of a daily gratitude journal.

Having survived numerous tragedies, including the deaths of his wife, mother, father, sister-in-law, and a number of very close friends, David has the real life experiences to encourage people to never give up.

His enthusiastic energy and passion for gratitude consistently delivers a message that any life, however difficult, can be lived to the fullest by utilizing several simple steps every day. That message becomes an extremely healthy coping mechanism to empower you every single day.

David George Brooke, aka, The Brooker, has been a speaker, author, and motivator for over 25 years. He specializes in coaching people to cope and manage the stresses of life by applying an ***attitude of gratitude***. To access his strategies on how to utilize your Daily Gratitude Journal, visit: http://www.thebrooker.com

David George Brooke

Made in the USA
San Bernardino, CA
06 May 2014